Outtakes has to do with two very important things in your life. One, any problem that you may have and two, God's Word. **Outtakes** is here to show you how to take any of your problems to God's Word and take out an answer.

God wants you to be at peace with yourself, your Creator, your family, and your world. **Outtakes** meets you where you are (sometimes hurting and sometimes happy) and shows you how to seek God's advice in all you do.

BY **Bill Sanders:**

Tough Turf
*(Almost) Everything Teens Want Parents to Know**
   **But Are Afraid to Tell Them*
Outtakes: Devotions for Girls
Outtakes: Devotions for Guys

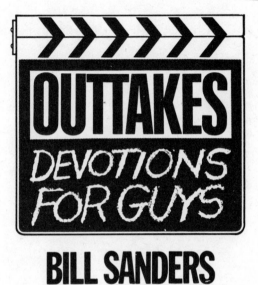

OUTTAKES
DEVOTIONS FOR GUYS

BILL SANDERS

Power Books

Fleming H. Revell
Old Tappan, New Jersey

Unless otherwise identified, Scripture texts are from the Holy Bible, New International Version, copyright © 1973. 1978, 1984 International Bible Society. Used by permission of Zondervan Bible Publishers.

Scripture quotations identified KJV are from the King James Version of the Bible.

Verses marked TLB are taken from The Living Bible, Copyright © 1971 by Tyndale House Publishers, Wheaton, Ill. Used by permission.

Library of Congress cataloging-in-Publication Data

Sanders, Bill, date
    Outtakes : devotions for guys / Bill Sanders.
       p. cm.
    ISBN 0-8007-5285-6
    1. Teenage boys—Prayer-books and devotions—English. I. Title.
BV4855.S26 1988   88-18197
242'.632—dc 19   CIP

Copyright © 1988 by Bill Sanders
Published by the Fleming H. Revell Company
Old Tappan, New Jersey 07675
Printed in the United States of America

To all the guys who have "been there" for me. You all helped me get through one of the toughest, yet beautiful, times in my life. I have just come through the death of my father, John W. Sanders. It was tough because I lost the greatest dad in the world, beautiful because I saw God take him out of his pain and into his new home, heaven. My dad died in peace because he knew Jesus as his personal Lord and Savior.

To my brother Dale: Thanks for being my special friend.

To my best friend, Kevin: You showed me that crying lasts but the night, and laughter truly does come in the morning.

To my friend and pastor, Will Davis: You've shown me by your word and example how to apply the wisdom of the Bible to my life, and you introduced its author to my dad. I'm forever grateful.

To Gary: Thanks for challenging me continually to develop a passion to be like Christ.

To Jon, Jim, Steve, Joe, Brian and Doug: Thanks for loving my dad and for crying and laughing with me.

Contents

Special Thanks

A special thanks goes to the students of the following schools for filling out hundreds of questionnaires. You gave us the needed information to identify the top problems you and your peers face. Thanks for your willingness and honesty.

Sandusky High School and Sandusky Middle School—Sandusky, Michigan
Westminster Academy—Fort Lauderdale, Florida
House of Hope—Orlando, Florida
Troy City Schools—Troy, Ohio
Mississinewa Community Schools—Gas City, Indiana
Holy Spirit School—Grand Rapids, Michigan
Holy Trinity School—Comstock Park, Michigan
Perrysburg Junior High School—Perrysburg, Ohio
Woodland Elementary—Perrysburg, Ohio
South Middle School and North Middle School—Joplin, Missouri
Croswell-Lexington Middle School—Croswell, Michigan
Pendleton Schools—Falmouth, Kentucky
Hool Elementary School and Heywood Elementary School—Troy, Ohio
Thanks also to the many kids who have written and shared their hurts and feelings with us.

Outtakes would never have been completed without my secretary, Kathy Reisner, and good friend Arla VanDusen's hard work reading through hundreds of students' letters, summarizing them, and compiling them for me. My mom read these letters as well and put them into categories so I could identify the greatest problems. Thanks, Mom. Sandy Bogema edited and put the finishing touches on many of the devotionals, with her thought-provoking one-liners and spiritual stimulators.

But this work would never have been completed had it not been for Kathy Reisner's spending literally hundreds of hours typing and retyping. She was also my constant encourager to stay on target. It's great having someone in my office who loves kids the way Kathy does.

1
True Friendships Are . . .

Friends are very special. When I was twenty years old, an old man told me, "You're a lucky person if you can go through life with your true friends on one hand with four fingers left over."

You are indeed fortunate to have a true-blue friend—not associates, not just people you know, but a true friend—one solid person who will never talk behind your back, always be there for you, and who knows how to listen as well as talk.

When I was seventeen, the words of my best friend, Steve, encouraged me. I was shy and self-conscious about being skinny, so I never wore shorts or short-sleeved shirts in public. Steve and I worked out in the hot sun; he tried to get me to wear shorts and take my shirt off, but I wouldn't. Then he said, "I know you have a hang-up about being skinny, but what you don't know is we're friends because of who you are on the inside, not what you look like on the outside." He could have scoffed at me, but instead he built me up.

What makes a great friend? Look and see if you possess any of the following characteristics. By practicing them, you may be able to put more than just one finger up when you count your friends.

15

1. *They accept you as you.* Like my friend Steve, true friends don't want you to pretend you are anyone but *you!*
2. *They challenge you spiritually.* I asked Josh McDowell who was his greatest mentor. He said Dick Day, because he kept him spiritually accountable and growing through everything he did.
3. *They are available.* They are there when you need them.
4. *They are great listeners.* Good friends want to hear from and about you. They always act as if they would rather be with you than anywhere in the world.
5. *They need you.* They need your friendship and encouragement, and it's easy for them to say so. You're not a crutch, but you lift them with your love.
6. *They are faithful.* They would never talk behind your back or make you look bad, no matter whom they are with.

I just returned from helping my friend Gary move two bookshelves. We talked and listened and comforted each other concerning some stressful areas in our lives. As we ended our short time together, we challenged each other to memorize one verse a week for the next year. As I returned to finish this devotion I realized that we covered all six of the points I had just written out.

Proverbs 17:17:   A friend loves at all times. . . .

Proverbs 18:24:   A man of many companions may come to ruin, but there is a friend who sticks closer than a brother.

Take a moment to see these two verses in action as you read 2 Samuel 1:26. David is not saying that his love for Jonathan is superior to marital love or that there is any sexual implication. He is calling attention to Jonathan's total commitment to his friendship. Be a Jonathan to someone who needs you today.

2
A Special Letter

What if you were to come home after school and notice this letter on your bed?

Dear Friend:

I watched you as you got up this morning, and I hoped that you would talk to Me—even if it was just a few words, asking My opinion or thanking Me for something good that happened in your life yesterday—but I noticed you were too busy trying to find just the right outfit to wear to school. I waited again. When you ran around the house, getting ready for school, I knew there would be a few minutes for you to stop and say hello to Me, but you were too busy. At one point you even had to wait for fifteen minutes, with nothing to do except sit in a chair. Then I saw you spring to your feet. I thought you wanted to talk to Me, but you ran to the phone and called a friend to ask about something that was happening later that day.

I watched you as you went to school, and I waited patiently all day long. With all your activities, I guess you were too busy to say anything to Me. I noticed that before lunch you looked around. Maybe you felt embarrassed to talk to Me, and that is why you didn't bow your head. You glanced three or four tables over in the cafeteria, and you noticed some of your friends talking to Me briefly before they ate, but you didn't. That's okay. There is still more time left, and I have hope that you will talk to Me even yet.

You went home, and it seems as if you had a lot of things to do. After a few of them were done, you turned on the TV. I don't know if I like TV or not. Just about anything goes there, and you spend a lot of time each day in front of it—not thinking about anything, but just enjoying the show. I wait patiently as you watch your TV and eat your meal, but again you don't talk to Me. People seem to come and go, but so few have time for Me. As you did your homework I waited. Again, you did what you had to do.

At bedtime I guess tonight you felt too tired. After you said good night to your family, you flopped into bed and fell asleep in no time. That's okay, because you may not realize that I am your special friend. I've got patience—more than you will ever know. I even want to teach you how to be patient with others as well. Because I love you so much, a long time ago I left a wonderful place called heaven and came to earth. I gave up heaven to be ridiculed and made fun of, and I even died so you wouldn't have to take My place. I love you so much that I will wait every day for a nod, a prayer, a thought, or a thankful part of your heart. I love you so, and I just want you to know that I want to be your special friend. It is hard when it is only a one-sided conversation and friendship. Well, you are getting up again, and I will wait again patiently, with nothing but love for you, hoping that today you will give Me some time. Have a nice day!

Your friend,
Jesus

If you are like me, Jesus could write that letter to you many days out of the year. Don't let Him write it today or tomorrow. Think about Him. Put Him in your plans, thoughts, and studies. *How would Jesus handle this? Thank You, Lord, for helping me through this.* Look up and say, "You did it again. You sure are my special friend." Ask Him to help with your memory skills (homework or Scripture); ask Him to give you the strength to call and make up with a friend, congratulate someone you don't know, or meet a new person. You can do it. Your special friend is waiting to help. He's already told you that in Matthew 28:20 (KJV), ". . . Lo, I am with you alway. . . ." Even if your name isn't *Lo,* Jesus is with you always!

3
The Greatest Amateur Athlete

It is called the Sullivan Award, and each year, the Amateur Athletic Union gives one to the country's top amateur athlete. In 1988 the ten finalists included such superstars as David Robinson (the NBA's number-one draft choice from Navy), Greg Foster (the world-record-holder indoor-hurdles champion), Janet Evans (world-record swimmer), and Kelcie Banks (the only United States boxer to win a medal at the Pan American games). Who would emerge on top? More than 2,000 reporters, amateur sport officials, and previous winners selected the finalist. They chose Jim Abbott—the University of Michigan's star baseball pitcher.

Jim is the first athlete from Michigan and the first baseball player ever to win the Sullivan Award, and he is no stranger to awards. Last fall he won the Golden Spikes Award, which goes to the best amateur baseball player in the country. In the Pan American games, in the summer of 1987, Jim made the United States baseball team and was selected to carry the American flag during the opening ceremonies. After that he won the Academy Awards of Sports honor for courage. Last winter the Philadelphia Sports Writers Association awarded him the Most Courageous Athlete honor. The United States Olympic Committee selected him as baseball player of the year. In his sophomore year at the University of Michigan, his record was 11–3, with a 2.08 earned-run average, and he was a third-team All-American. Then Jim was a part of Team USA. He went 8–1 with a 1.70 ERA. He was also the first American pitcher to beat Cuba, in Cuba, in twenty-five years. He pitched the United States team to a victory over Canada, assuring the United States of a silver medal in the Pan Am Games and a spot in the 1988 Summer Olympics

You probably think Jim Abbott is just like any othe superjock in your school: He has always had it handed to him on a silver platter, and he's been born with a gift of coordination, speed, the ability to pitch and think quickly. Well, part of that is right. But I haven't told you why Jim Abbott had to work harder than anyone else in school. He had to work harder at reaching his goals than you may ever have had to, because Jim Abbott was born with no right hand. He does it all with one normal arm and hand and another arm with no hand at all. Hard work, dedication, effort, and using his God-given talents and abilities have taken Jim Abbott to the top.

Each one of us has handicaps; every single person has to

overcome obstacles and shortcomings. What is it for you? Do you concentrate on your problems, or do you focus on the goal? Do you work hard and prepare and work harder when times get tough? Do you have ambition to really be something and do something with your God-given talents and abilities? Or do you cry whenever you fall and scrape a knee or someone laughs and makes fun of you? You must choose between two ways to go through this world: Use what God has given you, or abuse it and finally lose it.

By Jim's story, I'm inspired to be the best that I can be. My goal is to do a mighty work for God in public high schools across this country, never to be ashamed to share where I get my strength. By the way, since I've been sharing with student assembly groups how proud I am to be a Christian and that no one can take it away from me and that I get my strength from God and God alone (not my biorhythm and not my horoscope), the evening crowd, consisting of parents, doubled and tripled. It is no matter of coincidence either. God will supply us with our every need, if we only give Him the glory and use what He has given us.

Maybe you are not a star pitcher, maybe you will never play in the Pan Am Games or go to the Olympics, but look closely at what you've been given. Use it to the best of your ability. Though you may not stand under the bright lights, like Jim Abbott, you *can* feel a bright light shining in your heart if you do your very best with what you've been given. Get to work!

When Jesus was on earth, he called another man with very little talent to do what He wanted: Matthew, a despised and hated tax collector.

Mark 2:14: As he walked along, he saw Levi [his given name was Levi, but his apostolic name was *Matthew*, which means "gift of the Lord"] son of Alphaeus sitting at the tax collector's booth. "Follow me," Jesus told him, and Levi got up and followed him.

Matthew immediately followed. He took along his pen—the only thing he had. Later he wrote about the greatest life that was ever lived: He wrote about Jesus, and His story in the Gospel of Matthew.

Be like Jim Abbott and Matthew. Look at what God has given you and start pitching home runs. You can do it! (You can always trust God; he'll never throw you any curves.)

4

The Most Important Decisions of Your Life

Between the ages of seventeen and twenty-three you will make many of the most important decisions of your life. Most likely you will decide who you will marry, what profession you will enter, what education you will have, if you will become an alcoholic or an abuser of drugs and chemicals, and who your close friends will be. Many of your lifelong habits will become ingrained during these vital years.

During this time, most young people go to college or start a career. They get a job and their own apartments. Often they also fall away from God.

In addition young people may fall away from their

parents. Just out of high school, they want to become independent. He wants to be on his own, so he moves away. She feels angry at her parents for telling her what to do; she thinks they've pushed her around and never given her thoughts of her own or freedom or trust, so she goes out and sows her wild oats. Both teens discover the world.

Many young people make major decisions during these years, without their parents' or God's help—only to find themselves married. In their early twenties they have marriage problems, self-esteem problems, work problems, and maybe even a first divorce—not to mention drugs, alcohol, and so on.

Include God and your parents during these most vital and important years, I beg of you. Don't do it alone! Life is too tough alone, especially when you have to make decisions that will affect you the rest of your life. Having sex during these years could result in a pregnancy and an abortion and many memories that will never leave you.

Driving too fast without seat belts, using drugs, and so forth can all cause scars that will never fade. Be smart about it, and don't make these decisions without your parents—and most important, the Lord.

Going it alone merely shows that you are like everyone else. Life is too important and you are too special to try to handle it by yourself. If you act on only seventeen or twenty years of experience, the people whom you contact throughout your lifetime will never be touched in a special way. Use the wisdom of God and the wisdom and experience from your parents. God wants to lead the way for you—especially during these difficult years.

Proverbs 6:22, 23: When you walk, they will guide you; when you sleep, they will watch over you; when you awake, they will speak to you. For these commands are a lamp, this teaching is a light, and the corrections of discipline are the way to life.

Psalms 119:9: How can a young man keep his way pure? By living according to your word.

Joshua 1:8: Do not let this Book of the Law depart from your mouth; meditate on it day and night, so that you may be careful to do everything written in it. Then you will be prosperous and successful.

If you are hurting from a past mistake or need God near for a present decision you must make, call on God as the psalmist did in Psalms 102:1, 2: "Hear my prayer, O Lord; let my cry for help come to you. Do not hide your face from me when I am in distress. Turn your ear to me; when I call, answer me quickly."

5

Who's Pressuring Whom?

Call it peer pressure, if you want; but it's not, because it has nothing to do with your peers. It's one of the four types of pressure people label "peer pressure"—I call it "me pressuring me" pressure. The other three types are:

1. "Follow the crowd" pressure.
2. "Can't be me" pressure.
3. "Afraid to try" pressure.

These four are discussed in detail, along with fifteen ways to avoid harmful pressures, in my book *Tough Turf*.

What is "me pressuring me" pressure? It's when you have braces and won't smile. Not smiling becomes a habit (a permanent pattern), and you don't smile after the orthodontist takes them off, either. It's the guy who talks himself out of asking the girl of his dreams out for a date. It's someone getting Cs instead of A's, because she sees herself as average instead of a top achiever.

Answer these questions yes or no.

Are you afraid to pray while on a date?
Are you afraid to wear your seat belt if nonusers are in the car?
Is it hard to tell your parents you love them?
Do you raise your hand in class, if you have a question?

Who really pressures you to act the way you do in situations like these? It's usually you. To combat this, fill yourself with God's love and wisdom by digging into His Word. Your mind will be renewed, and your heart will be filled with new courage and conviction for God and His way. Everyday pressures that devastate most young people will become child's play for you.

Take a few moments and memorize this verse:

James 4:17: Anyone, then, who knows the good he ought to do and doesn't do it, sins.

6
Winners or Losers

Please pay close attention. These are true statements: *You were not born a winner. You were not born a loser. You were born a chooser.* Winners and losers we are not, but choosers we most definitely are. Don't be like sheep: Suppose you saw one hundred sheep in a row, jumping over a gate. What would happen to the rest of the sheep if partway through the line you took down the gate? That's right! The rest would keep jumping over the gate, even though it was no longer there. Sheep were not born winners, losers, or choosers; they were just born dumb. They cannot lead, only follow. Because they cannot think for themselves, sheep do not have freedom of choice. But you do, and so do I.

Decide for yourself what and how you are going to choose. Each day is packed with one decision after another. You start out with deciding what time to get up, what to wear, what to eat, where to go, who to go with, and the list goes on. Throughout each day, each week, each year, consciously or subconsciously, you'll make many small and big decisions. But small decisions usually set the stage for big decisions. For example, one seemingly small decision to take one drug, one time, could impact many large decisions. I have a friend who took one drug, one time, and many big life decisions were answered for her. She will never have to decide on a job, a spouse, a college, children, anything—she will live out life as a "mental vegetable," in the care of her parents or a guardian. Her small choice changed her life forever—in a major way.

God didn't produce robots. He made people. Aren't you glad your life isn't programmed on a floppy disk? I am. Jesus also is a chooser. He chose to love you and me—and even die—as a sacrifice for our sins, to build a permanent bridge between God the Father and us. This is what Jesus says about himself. Read John 10:7–9.

John 10:9: "I am the gate; whoever enters through me will be saved. He will come in and go out, and find pasture."

7

Is It Really Cheating?

Dear Bill: I've heard it said that when you cheat on a test, you really cheat yourself. Do you really think that if a student looks over on another person's paper for just an answer or two out of an entire test, he is really hurting himself?

When I was in college, I took a management course—one I had to have to earn a business degree. This was a large lecture class with several hundred students. Each week we had to take a quiz. Throughout the semester the professor gave twelve to fifteen quizzes. You had to take at least 80 percent of them. Out of every ten quizzes, you could miss a couple.

One time, I was leaving town for the weekend with some friends. As I walked off campus, a classmate from this class came up and asked me if I would be at class that day. I told him no, I was leaving for the weekend.

"I'll be glad to take the quiz for you," he offered.

"No, that's okay."

"Really. No problem. Just give me your student I.D. number, and I'll take the quiz for you. I'll put your name and number on it and hand it in at the end of the class."

My first mistake was not thinking about his offer and thinking through my answer. My second mistake, probably a greater one, was not having integrity and honesty so built into my system that I wouldn't even have to think about such a ridiculous question. Since I was the king of my life during those days and listened to no one but myself and made many bad decisions because God was not guiding me (nor did I want Him to), I looked my classmate in the eye and said, "Sure. . . . Go ahead and do it. Here is my I.D. number."

I didn't even have to take that test. But I didn't really consider it cheating, because I didn't do anything. Oh, sure, I gave him consent, but he was going to do everything. Besides, he told me he had it all thought out and would take care of it. There wasn't even a professor in the room—just hundreds of students and a box in the back, where the tests went at the end of the hour. I figured it was a cinch and guaranteed to work.

A week later, after class was over, the professor announced he wanted to see Bill Sanders and the other fellow. We both walked into his office. He put both test papers on the table and said, "Both of you cheated." We acted innocent and said, "What do you mean?" He said, "Look. Both papers are identical." He also showed me where the other guy had written his name and I.D. on his paper—and on my paper he wrote his name, crossed it off, and put my name above it. It was very obvious what had happened.

The professor said, "Guess what both of you get to do?"

We asked, "What?"

"You get to take this class over again next year: This year you receive Fs. That will bring your grade-point averages down; it will be on your record that you got this F because of cheating; and this will go into your major and be on your college record forever."

I learned a very valuable lesson that day. First I learned that some friends are not really friends at all, because they don't even stand on sound principles. I also learned about the word *cheating*. I tried to justify that I wasn't really cheating and he was doing it for me, and there was no way we could get caught because he had it all figured out. It is like the story I hear from young people who get caught with drugs, driving too fast, or drinking while they are driving. Their friends seem to have it all figured out: "There is no way we can get caught. I've thought about it ahead of time." Baloney. Cheating is cheating. Cheating hurts you by tearing at your insides. It makes you realize that you are not really a great person. You would stoop to cheating or anything else to help yourself—no right or wrong, no morals, no "God's rules," just do your own thing. If it feels good, don't worry if you hurt anyone, and don't get caught.

You *do* hurt yourself if you cheat. I had to take the class over again, and the second time I got a B. Put a B and an F together, and it averages out to be a D. I realized that it just was not worth it.

Honesty and integrity are things you can't buy—and people cannot take them from you. If someone asks you if you want to cheat or be a part of something you know is wrong, without a moment's hesitation, say, "Absolutely not.

I am not going to compromise my values or myself for this, so I say *no*."

I had a very costly lesson, and I hope you don't have to go through it. The next time you take a test and your eyes start to wander, remember that you will definitely hurt yourself. You might not get caught the way I did, but you will live with a broken part of yourself on the inside for a long time. It is just not worth it.

When you feel tempted to copy or cheat, remember that you are actually imitating the person you are copying:

3 John 11: Dear friend, do not imitate what is evil but what is good. Anyone who does what is good is from God. Anyone who does what is evil has not seen God.

Ephesians 5:1: Be imitators of God. . . .

If you want to copy someone, I think God's Word clearly shows who that should be!

8
My Way

Have you ever heard Frank Sinatra or Elvis Presley sing the song "My Way"? If you have, you've heard the words and know it says we control our own lives: I'm proud of how I handled things; through life's highs and lows, I did everything my way. You know, there is a lot of truth in that. Not that it is the right way, necessarily, but there it holds a lot of truth.

We have only two ways to do things—God's way or "my way." My way can be influenced by many things: God; the world; Satan; people who hate life and God; the good, bad, and indifferent. Whenever we go through life saying, "I do things my way," we are shortsighted and not very wise. Doing things God's way gives us a much better chance at coming out in the end and being happy, peaceful, and handling life as God wants us to. Remember, God created us; He created life itself; He gave us the rules; He gave us some fantastic principles; He gave us people to look at and listen to; and He gave us many examples in His Bible to tell us how to do it right and how to do it wrong. Look at people who did it their way and watch how they struggle, have shame, pain, bitterness, hate, and envy for the rest of their lives. You can see people who end in ruin or happiness. In the end you have to ask yourself, *Whose way will I do things?*

Isaiah 55:8,9: "For my thoughts are not your thoughts, neither are your ways my ways," declares the Lord. "As the heavens are higher than the earth, so are my ways higher than your ways and my thoughts than your thoughts."

Psalms 119:173: May your hand be ready to help me, for I have chosen your precepts.

David, the psalmist, chose God's way. Ask yourself, *Which way have I chosen to live: my way or His way?*

9
Just Your Ears

Dear Mom and Dad: Don't you understand that I need you even more when I *don't* succeed? You love to claim me as yours when I do things right. It would be nice if you could come out of your own world and could just open up and listen to me just once.

Being a parent myself, I know how hard it is to merely listen. Parents find it easy to give commands, yell, and even hit, if their kids don't immediately respond as they want them to. Sometimes we parents forget that our children should truly be guests in our home. When the stresses get high, it is very easy to let that slip.

Have you ever felt as if your parents loved you more when you succeeded and looked good in their eyes, than when you did an average job or failed at something? Think about what's going on then! When things go well, you find it easy to feel happy, and it's the same with your parents. So they just naturally treat you better when you do something well.

Share the right way to listen with your parents, and listen yourself, too. Listening means more than sitting still without saying anything. Body language is very important when you listen. Facing the person, arms open (not crossed with tight lips and your head down) tells the speaker you want to hear. He can read the very way your eyes look. Have an expression on your face that says, *I'm interested in you. I love you. Please tell me more!*

When a child comes to them with a problem or concern parents need to learn to keep their mouths shut. We have been given two ears and one mouth, and parents should use them in that proportion, so their son or daughter knows they really care and understand. All of us find that when someone butts in and talks while we are talking, we get the distinct impression that they do not know what we are talking about. When we listen to people, we shouldn't keep looking over their shoulders and watching who else comes into the room. We should concentrate on them.

If you need to talk to your parents, sit against the wall, so they cannot look beyond you. In a cafeteria, a restaurant, or even at home, but especially in public, place yourself so they cannot look beyond you. Next, concentrate on their eyes. Don't keep looking around the room. Teenagers and young people in this day and age find it hard to keep eye contact. I am not exactly sure why, but I think it is a problem of self-worth and reflects the feeling, *I've never been taught how to look people in the eye, and maybe I'm not worth it.* You are worth it; so are your relationships.

These ideas take time, effort, and energy; but they also last a lifetime. Not only can they keep your relationship strong with your parents, they also work with your future mate, friends, employers, and co-workers. If you wish they would listen to you more and appreciate you, no matter what, go to your mom and dad. Tell them how very important it is, when you come to them with a problem, for them to merely understand and be there. After you speak up, they can help you find a solution. Tell them to never give up—with God all things are possible.

If I have learned anything from writing this book, it is that in God's Word there is an answer for everything we've faced, a way to defeat every fear, anxiety, depression, and attack of Satan. In God's Word there is hope. You can find it, too.

Your challenge for the day: If your parents don't listen the way they should or the way you wish they would, please show them what real success in God's eyes is. You'll find it in Psalm 1.

Psalms 1:2, 3: But his delight is in the law of the Lord, and on his law he meditates day and night. He is like a tree planted by streams of water, which yields its fruit in season and whose leaf does not wither. Whatever he does prospers.

Show your parents that we all have our season to yield fruit and be a success. Tell them that this is your off-season. Use your sense of humor and turn your parents to God's Word. Together you will become closer than you've ever imagined.

10
Don't Fry Your Brain

Drug abuse is on the rise in America. In some high schools, alcohol affects 80 to 90 percent of the young people. Before you make choices regarding drugs, chemicals, and alcohol, consider these facts:

Drugs short-circuit the thinking process.

Sixty percent of fatally injured teenage drivers were found to have alcohol in their blood systems.

Eleven teenagers die each day in drunk-driving accidents.

Drinking, doping, and driving don't mix.

Dual use of pot and alcohol is addictive. They increase each other's strength, doubling the impairment.

Tobacco smoking is the largest preventable cause of death in America. Studies now show that pot is even more harmful.

Pot destroys a driver's ability to realize and respond to danger.

Life expectancy has improved in the United States for every age group but one—the years between fifteen and twenty-four. The higher death rate among that age group is due to drunk drivers.

Each day 360 teenagers are injured in alcohol- or drug-related accidents.

Do these seem like a bunch of facts that don't mean anything? Is the student four lockers down from you, who has a drug or an alcohol problem, just another statistic that doesn't mean anything to anyone in this busy world? I hope not. Today, look around. Try to make this world a better place. Challenge someone with a chemical or alcohol problem to talk to a counselor about it.

Teenagers who use dope are the dopes. Don't be one. You are too wise, and God has wonderful things planned for you. Let Him work in your life.

1 Thessalonians 5:15:   Make sure that nobody pays back wrong for wrong, but always try to be kind to each other and to everyone else.

Be an "overcomer"; don't "come over" to worldly pleasures. It's no fun to die!

11
Ability Versus Availability

Dear Bill: After hearing you give a talk at our school, I have a question to ask you. I am so very average. How in the world can I ever do a great thing and reach my potential, as you said in your talk? Is it really possible for people of average intelligence, coordination, and so on, like myself, to really do great things, or was it just part of your talk?

Dear Mr. Average: I am so glad you brought this question to my attention, because it is on the hearts of almost everyone. We each look around and see people who seem much more talented, more beautiful, and who have more things going for them than we seem to have going for us. Most of us don't even ask the questions you have: *Can I do great things? Can I really be something special in this world? Can I really make a difference?*

The answer is a definite yes!

I'd like to show you an example in God's Word that highlights the difference between what you can do with your own ability and what availability to God will make happen.

In Exodus 3 we read about Moses and the burning bush. God told Moses this was holy ground. He said, "I am the God of your father, the God of Abraham, the God of Isaac and the God of Jacob"(v.6). In Exodus 3:10 he continues: "So now, go. I am sending you to Pharaoh to bring my people the Israelites out of Egypt."

Like many of us, when we feel something great is at hand, but do not feel capable of doing it, Moses asked, "Who am I . . . ?" (v. 11). Notice how God replied: Exodus 3:12, "I will be with you. . . ." All He wanted was for Moses to make himself available. Moses didn't think he had many abilities. In Exodus 4:10, 11, Moses said to the Lord, "O Lord, I have never been eloquent, neither in the past nor since you have spoken to your servant. I am slow of speech and tongue." Just like you, Moses was afraid of speech class. The Lord said to him, "Who gave man his mouth? Who makes him deaf or dumb? Who gives him sight or makes him blind? Is it not I, the Lord?" God says, "If you are only available, I will be with you." Exodus 4:15 says of Moses and his brother Aaron: ". . . I will help both of you speak and will teach you what to do."

If you only become available to Him, with a heart tuned in to doing good, right, touching lives, and living by integrity and honesty, God will lead the way. He will open the doors and even move your tongue and heart. He will give you a tender conscience. You will know right from wrong and what to do and how to do it. No longer will you wonder how to carry your light, but you have to put God in the center of your heart and your life before you can hear Him calling and leading you.

12
Whose Fault Is It?

I receive letter after letter from teens across America, sharing how they feel as if they are a nothing or a nobody because of their past. Maybe they have been abused by their parents; maybe they have turned to drugs in order to handle a terrible home situation—sometimes it's because of incest or rape. Young people carry such scars for a lifetime. Ask yourself, "Whose fault is it?"

Please realize that if your mom and dad have a bad relationship, it's not your fault. It's not your fault that so much junk goes on in this world, that there's so much misunderstanding, that there are so many broken homes. It's not your fault if your parents never knew exactly how to listen to you or get tuned in to your feelings or encourage you to talk.

The next time you feel bad about the way your life has gone, realize that you have to take responsibility for some things—your actions and reactions—but you don't have to take responsibility for the situation in your home or how you grew up as a child. If you can separate the two, you will find it easier to realize that with God's help you can make it in this world. You can make it in this thing called life. God does give hope. Don't place on yourself the added pressure and weight of the guilt that goes along with the things that weren't your fault in the first place. Have a super day and think on the good things. Soar over bad situations with the Savior.

Isaiah 40:29–31: He gives strength to the weary and increases the power of the weak. Even youths grow tired and weary, and young men stumble and fall; but those who hope in the Lord will renew their strength. They will soar on wings like eagles; they will run and not grow weary, they will walk and not be faint.

13
Different Standards for Guys and Girls?

Seventeen hundred high-school kids in a jammed-packed auditorium listen to my friend John Crudele, "Just Say *No*" expert, speak. He asks the girls, "What do you call a guy who has had sex several times?" He makes sure that they answer him, and they say something like, "A stud," or, "A hunk."

Then he goes to the guys and says, "What do you call a girl who has had sex several times? Come on . . . I want to know." Most of the guys sit there and don't say anything, but he persists: "Tell me. What do you call a girl who has had sex several times, and the word is out around school that she's been around a little bit?" Finally he gets some brave ones who say, "Do you really want us to tell you?" He says, "Yes, I want to know right now." Then they say, "A sleaze," or, "A slut."

John says, "You've got it. Isn't that the way it goes? Look, girls. Realize what is being done here and what is being said. If a guy has been around a little bit with other girls, he is made out to be a hero and the big shot on campus; but any girl who messes around and has sex before marriage is considered a slut or a whore. These statements should make you sick to your stomach for trying to keep up with peer pressure."

Then John asks the guys, "How many times would you want your future wife to have had sex with other people before you marry her—one, two, three, four, five times? If you become a parent and have a daughter, how many times would you want her to have sex before she gets married—three, five, ten times? How many? How about your mother, guys? How many times would you want her to have had sex before she had sex with your father . . . five, ten, fifteen, twenty? How many?" All of a sudden an entire audience of young people, for the first time in their lives, may get hit between the eyes with the fact that God says premarital sex is wrong, and it hurts you if you do it. There is no right way to have sex before marriage. You cannot have "safe sex," because nothing will save you from the low self-esteem, the memories that haunt your mind for the rest of your life, as you compare your wife or husband with all your previous lovers. You are not safe from the facts that condoms do not protect you from many venereal diseases, that AIDS is 100 percent deadly, that Dr. Ruth does not care about your life and is not standing on any moral principles whatsoever, and that just because Planned Parenthood says everyone does it, I say, "So what?" They are talking just as Satan would if he were talking to you. I challenge you to greatness. I challenge you to be worth waiting for.

When will the world wake up? When are you, as a young

person with a life ahead of you, going to realize that what you do today puts a scar on your mind forever? Memories don't go away; quite often they last a lifetime, haunting and belittling us. They give us guilt and pain. You can avoid that by standing on God's principles today. Don't give in just because everyone else does. Don't *be* everyone else!

Guys, if you think you are a stud or the cool dude around campus because you have been around a little bit and had sex with women, look at one of the strongest men in the whole Bible—Samson. He was God's hero for a moment, but he lusted after beautiful women who had nothing to do with God. They were unrighteous, but he didn't care. His hormones and his desire to fulfill his feelings caused him and the entire nation to suffer because he tried to satisfy his inner feelings, desires, and motives, instead of thinking about right and wrong—what God desired.

Read Judges 16 to find out where Samson's weakness really lay. It wasn't in losing his hair, but in being enticed by a woman because of lust. Delilah tricked Samson three different times, and Samson had become so blind to her tricks that he never suspected that she would do it again. Following our desires does that to us: We get blind, we follow no matter what, we forget about God and all the pain that will lie ahead of us.

Judges 16:4, 16, 17, 19, 21: Some time later, he fell in love with a woman in the Valley of Sorek whose name was Delilah. . . . With such nagging she prodded him day after day until he was tired to death. So he told her everything. "No razor has ever been used on my head," he said, "because I have been a Nazirite set apart to God since birth. If my head were shaved, my strength would leave me, and I would become as weak as any other man." . . . Having put him to sleep on her lap, she called a man to shave off the seven braids of his hair, and so began to subdue him. And his strength left him. . . . Then the Philistines seized him, gouged out his eyes and took him down to Gaza. Binding him with bronze shackles, they set him to grinding in the prison.

14
A Wounded Bird Still Flies High

What is it like to be Larry Bird? The February 24, 1988 issue of *USA Today* inspired me with an article on one of athletics' greatest heroes. Two of his fingers are so smashed up that he can't straighten them out. After every game he has to soak his Achilles tendons in ice buckets to ease the pain. Now his nose is broken. He has scrapes and bald spots all over his body, where he has left skin on gym floors across this country when he has dived for balls. He is wounded, but not down and out. In fact, he may have his best season ever. He is the third in NBA in scores, with a 29.7 average. He also averages 9.7 rebounds and 6.1 assists. He shoots an unbelievable 53 percent from the field and 91 percent from the foul line. Under pressure, many experts consider him the game's best three-point shooter, at 41 percent.

Bird doesn't like to talk much about his injuries. He just likes to play, and play hard he does. Before every game he goes out to shoot by himself for two and one-half hours. In fact, he's practiced so hard with his left hand that within ten feet of the basket he is just as effective with it as with his right. He is also known as one of the most unselfish players in the NBA. At times he hasn't shot for an entire period because he was trying to get other team members involved in the offense.

Detroit coach Chuck Daily says, "He's better than ever." His teammate Danny Ainge says, "Larry's lost weight. He's better . . . better than ever before." Since the all-star break, in the last eight games Larry Bird has averaged 35.6 points, and that includes the game in which he broke his nose. He only had thirteen points in that one. If you left that game out, his average would be 38.9. Along with Michael Jordan and Magic Johnson, Bird is one of the top three to be considered for this year's most valuable player. This kind of hustle, persistence, and dedicated work has already earned him three previous MVP awards.

In the off-season, most players rest a bit when they don't have to come to practice. On the other hand, Larry worked mighty hard preparing for this season, when very few other players practiced and worked out. He went on an extensive conditioning program. He's trimmer and quicker than ever.

What are you and I doing to perfect our skills? Whether it is baseball, playing the trumpet, studying chemistry, helping out in our communities, or making our church youth group the best ever, what are we doing to continually better our best? We can learn from Larry Bird, and we can also learn about stick-to-it-iveness, determination, and using our God-given talents from a very small member of the insect kingdom: the ant. Scripture talks extensively about the ant. Let's learn a lesson from it as we head off to conquer today and be our best and touch the world for Christ.

Proverbs 6:6–11:   Go to the ant, you sluggard; consider its ways and be wise! It has no commander, no overseer or ruler, yet it stores its provisions in summer and gathers its food at harvest. How long will you lie there, you sluggard? When will you get up from your sleep? A little sleep, a little slumber, a little folding of the hands to rest—

Proverbs 30:24–28: "Four things on earth are small, yet they are extremely wise: Ants are creatures of little strength, yet they store up their food in the summer; conies are creatures of little power, yet they make their home in the crags; locusts have no king, yet they advance together in ranks; a lizard can be caught with the hand, yet it is found in kings' palaces."

15
Sick and Tired

I don't know about you, but I get sick and tired of people scoffing at me because of my beliefs. Recently I visited a nice restaurant with my wife and another couple. The waitress came over and asked us if we wanted any drinks before the meal. We all said no, and she said, "You really don't want any drinks?" We said, "No. We are perfectly content." Then she gave us that look and a little bit of a chuckle that implied, *How do you expect to have fun without any drinks?* She acted as if we were the weird ones. A few days after that a business associate of mine and I went to lunch and the very same thing occurred.

I hear the same scoop from young people in schools. A Christian came up to me in a public school and shared how the guys give him grief because he has never had sex with a girl. He said, "The pressure is unbelievable. They make me feel as if I am the creep and I am doing wrong, because I respect girls and don't take advantage of them when I take them out." Realize that many people in this world want us to be just like them, because that way they have no competition. If everyone does what they do, they won't have to feel bad about their way of life.

I'm proud of the fact that one of my greatest accomplishments was not speaking with President Ford or President Reagan, sharing my thoughts before a crowd of almost 7,000, speaking in front of some 10,000 kids a week, several weeks a year, or being nominated for the Gold Medallion Award for my book *Tough Turf*. It was when I dumped my entire liquor stock down the toilet. I have been proud ever since to say that I choose not to drink. It was also a proud moment when I helped my brother pour all of his down his toilet. The bottles were gone forever. The memories were still there, and so are the heartaches and pain, but a new way of life is something that each one of us can change to and decide to do whenever we wish.

When someone offers you a drink and you tell them you're a nondrinker, don't be ashamed. Don't feel embarrassed if you are the only one who doesn't smoke cigarettes. How can they make smoking out to be so glamorous? It is one of the most disgusting things I've ever seen. Of course, the ads never tell you about the smelly clothes, the yellow teeth, the bad breath, and how everyone can tell you smoke when you walk into a crowd. Smoking also says a lot about our self-worth and the way we feel about ourselves.

No matter what you stand for or against, remember that there are two groups of people—those who believe in and follow God's way, and those who believe in and walk in the world's way. I really am sick and tired of people acting as if you're strange if you follow God's way. I guess that's my pet peeve, and I need to work through it, to try to forgive those people and not be so angry. I will, but I'm also never going to turn back, just because someone scoffs at me. I am going to take a lesson from God's Word about which way I should believe.

Luke 9:25: "What good is it for a man to gain the whole world, and yet lose or forfeit his very self?"

John 15:18, 19: "If the world hates you, keep in mind that it hated me first. If you belonged to the world, it would love you as its own. As it is, you do not belong to the world, but I have chosen you out of the world. That is why the world hates you."

16
It's Just a Job

Think of your friends who have jobs. Think of some of their parents. What attitudes do they possess toward their work? Some might say: "I need it to earn money and that's all," or, "It doesn't bother me to steal from my employer. He makes so much money on me and doesn't pay me very much in the first place," or, "I've got to go to my job, or I'll get fired," or, "Take this job and shove it."

People don't appreciate their employers much these days. A friend of mine owns a supermarket and told me about an employee who was found dealing drugs right in the store, while he was being paid a wage. Of course the employee got fired, of course he had a bad reputation in the area, and he absolutely would not get a good recommendation from my friend. If you are working for someone, is it just a job, or do you appreciate it? Do you come in early and work late? Do you call people by name? Do you learn as much as you can about the industry, business, and customers?

I remember the job I had in a supermarket. My goal was to be the fastest bagger there. Always with a smile, I called people by name and was always happy-go-lucky. As I flipped those cans from one hand to the other and into the sack over and over again, carried the bag out with a smile, opened the door for the people, packed the groceries neatly in the trunk, I would get very nice tips. I soon got moved up to the meat department. Before too long I had my own business. I never took it as a job. I remembered the day my brother had told me, "You are a good worker. Nobody can take that away from you. Don't let them!"

In Bible days many people had one everyday occupation: They were shepherds. Some of those shepherds believed taking care of their sheep was more than just a job. If they had one hundred sheep and one got lost, they went after the one. If the lost one had fallen over a stoney cliff in a dangerous spot, a dedicated shepherd would climb down the edge of the mountain and bring that one lost sheep back to safety. He would protect the sheep against wolves and other animals; he would stay up late at night and watch over them. It wasn't just a job for a few hours at a minimum wage, but he took it very seriously and treated it as an important position.

Someone in the Bible is called the Good Shepherd: He treats it as more than just a job, too. Jesus is His name, and watching over His sheep is His game. He loves us and does not want even one of us to stray or fall—to go to hell. Like a shepherd, He cares about us and wants to guide us through the pastures of life. Jesus wants to bring us to green pastures of living waters; He even said He is the living water. If we drink of Him, we will never again thirst. This means that if we have Christ in our hearts, what we truly need in life is already bought and paid for.

Let Jesus be your shepherd, and remember that on your job your employer believes in you and is paying you a good wage. *Profit* is not a dirty word. In fact, if your employer doesn't make a profit, he won't have a business, and you won't have a job. Give him your best. Give him your all. Let other people say, "I want you to work for me. If that guy doesn't give you a raise, come to me. I will give you one." Watch what happens when you treat your job as your own business—with excitement, enthusiasm, and respect. Be the best you can. *No one can do it for you.*

Besides, in the long run it is not just a job. Colossians 3:23 says, "Whatever you do, work at it with all your heart, as working for the Lord, not for men."

17

Can I Have the Car?

Have you ever noticed how the words that come out of your mouth cause your parents to wonder and guess what is going on in your life? Probably, you never really give them straightforward answers. For instance, you may like to keep them guessing—especially in a situation like asking for the car keys.

48

"Dad, is it okay if I borrow the car keys?"

"Where are you going?" he asks.

"Nowhere."

You come back from nowhere in about four hours. Your dad looks at the odometer: 492 miles. He comes into your room and says, "Where did you go tonight?"

Of course, you tell him, "Nowhere!"

"Who were you with tonight?"

"No one."

Then comes the big question: *What did you do?*

Like all your peers across this country, you say, "Nothing."

It is funny how every teen can go nowhere for such a long period of time and spend so much money with nobody and have so much fun doing nothing. Is it any wonder that parents ask teens where they are going and wonder how they are feeling when they say everything is okay, even though the parents can tell by the tone of the teen's voice and the way that he carries himself that he hurts and is dying to talk?

Proverbs 10:1:   A wise son brings joy to his father, but a foolish son grief to his mother.

Did you know that it is more profitable for you to make your father happy than to make your mother sad? You'll get along much better. Life will become a lot easier, and they might even help you on your homework from time to time!

Do one of the toughest things you'll ever have to during these teenage years. Really talk to your parents and communicate with them. If you hurt, let them know. If you know they don't understand you, go to them and say, "I know that you don't really know what is going on in my life. Can we sit down? I want you to know me better, and I want to know you better." This is not popular, and none of your other friends will do this, but you will see powerful and profitable results in your life. Face it, you have to live with your parents much more than your friends. Besides, as soon as you graduate from high school, you will end up knowing, relating to, and regularly seeing only one or two of your school friends. That is it. Three years after you are out of high school, if you still regularly see three or four people you graduated with, you are among only 5 percent of the young people in this country. Usually this will happen if you are in a small town and if you stay there—and so do your friends.

Your parents remain your parents forever. When you say things in code to try to keep them guessing and never let them know when you are hurt, you miss out on one of the greatest resources you have at your disposal—your parents! They love you more than anyone in the world, and they have all those years of wisdom and practical experience and totally caring about your best interest. Wisely tune into them and turn to them when you need help.

Sometimes you may keep your parents guessing at the end of a date as well. How long should a girl be allowed to stay in the car with her date before her father comes out? My father said as long as it takes them to turn off the ignition. One dad went out to the car and said, "It's time to come in." The daughter said, "Don't you trust me?" Her dad yelled, "No! I wouldn't even trust me out here under these circumstances."

Don't keep your mom and dad guessing. When your mom is inside, flashing the front light on and off, come on in. Do your conversation in the living room, instead of in the dark car. Don't put yourself in situations that could cause long-term heartache and pain. You owe it to yourself and your parents to tell them exactly what you are up to and how you hurt.

Mark 10:19: "You know the commandments: 'Do not murder, do not commit adultery, do not steal, do not give false testimony, do not defraud, honor your father and mother.'"

18
"Everyone Else Is"

> I have a problem with my parents. They don't care what I do. They say I can do anything and go anywhere, just as long as I don't get into trouble. My grades are suffering, and I need some guidelines. Help!

Can you imagine feeling like this—upset because your parents are giving you too much freedom? Many teens say, "Try me, try me"—except for the ones who have parents, like the girl who wrote this letter, who won't say no.

In my talks I tell young people they are very fortunate if they have parents who love them enough and have a strong enough relationship with them to say no. Most teens in the audience roll their eyes when I say this, but not the ones who have to make decisions all alone.

We all need a pilot in life. When we drive over a tall bridge, if we can see guard rails on each side, we feel more secure. We won't go close to them, but it feels good just having them there. Studies also show that in a divorce situation teens and preteens would rather live with the parent who is the firmest disciplinarian, with defined rules to follow. You might say they're looking for a pilot.

51

Are you one of the lucky ones? Do your parents say no? Do they explain why they are against this or that? If He meant you to go through these early years on your own, God wouldn't have given you parents.

What is known as the first commandment with a promise, and what is that promise? Look it up and find out. It's somewhere between Deuteronomy 5:6–16. Here's a hint! It's the fifth commandment. Notice God's specific promise to you.

Paul puts "disobeying parents" next to God haters and murderers in Romans 1:30, 31. If your parents are trying their best to train you for a life on your own, you may want to tell them, "Thanks for saying no."

Ephesians 6:1–4: Children, obey your parents in the Lord, for this is right. "Honor your father and mother"—which is the first commandment with a promise—"that it may go well with you and that you may enjoy long life on the earth."

Fathers, do not exasperate your children; instead, bring them up in the training and instruction of the Lord.

19
Too Much to Live For

Every now and then each of us gets a telephone call we wish we hadn't received—usually because we don't like to hear what the person has to say. A while back I got one of those calls from a friend, who shared a story of his friend's teenage son, who had just committed suicide.

The boy, who seemed to be a high achiever, went to a highly rated college. He appeared to have everything going for him, yet he took his own life. The day before he committed suicide, he made a simple everyday mistake. My friend explained that they think this boy had nothing to live for because he did not know how to tell his father that he had goofed up! My insides hurt while I listened and tried to help in any way I could, and I could only think that this boy had so much to live for. Even more I hurt at not knowing his spiritual condition.

Who's Who Among American High School Students recently conducted a survey dealing with high achievers and suicide. Of the 1,943 students surveyed, 31 percent of high school juniors and seniors who were high achievers had considered suicide.

The factors contributing most to suicides are:

Feelings of worthlessness	86%
Feelings of isolation and loneliness	81%
Pressure to achieve	72%
Fear of failure	61%
Communication gap with parents	58%
Drug and alcohol use	58%
Actual failure	56%
Lack of attention from parents	50%
Lack of stability in the family	49%
Fear for personal future	41%
Unwanted pregnancy	32%
Divorce	24%
Sexual problems	23%
Financial concerns	14%

Reprinted by permission from GROUP Magazine, copyright 1987, Thom Schultz Publications, Inc. Box 481, Loveland, CO 80539.

Of these fourteen factors, notice the one way up top . . . the feeling that I am worth nothing. Can't you see how most all of the rest of these problems directly relate to a person's self-esteem and feeling of worth?

You don't have to be part of these statistics. You've read the factual breakdown, but you don't have to "break down" as you live your life. Tomorrow we'll consider some of the other factors in more detail.

Romans 5:8:   But God demonstrates his own love for us in this: While we were still sinners, Christ died for us.

Jesus loves you so much that He died for you even when you were a sinner. God's love should give you great worth. Read the first three chapters of my book *Tough Turf* for step-by-step guides to raising your self-esteem.

20
Beyond Suicide

Here are some other factors that cause suicide: Zero in on your weakness, and take it to the Lord, who can make you strong!

Feelings of isolation and loneliness: You won't feel lonely or isolated if you like yourself, because you won't mind being with yourself.

Pressure to achieve: If you feel self-worth and enjoy a healthy self-esteem, you usually won't feel much pressure to achieve. You'll do your best and enjoy the day. You'll live for the moment—not tomorrow—and won't worry about yesterday, either.

Fear of failure: Never worry about failure, because it is just a part of life. Everyone fails at some things. Babe Ruth struck out more times than any other person in baseball at the same time that he held the record for the most home runs.

Communication gap with parents: If you feel good about yourself, you will communicate with your parents, because you will recognize that they have weaknesses in this area, too. You will understand that if you find talking to your parents difficult, it is also probably hard for them to listen to you or to talk back and share their concerns and worries.

Drug and alcohol use: If you like yourself, especially if you have Jesus Christ living in your heart, and believe that your body is truly a temple of the Lord, you won't put drugs and alcohol into your system. You would not want something to go into your body that will kill thousands of brain cells every instant.

Actual failure: Don't let it bother you a bit. It is a part of life.

Lack of attention from parents and stability in the family: This won't really bother you. If you want more attention from your parents, you might have to first give them some attention. If your family isn't stable, you can't take responsibility for your parents, but you can help add to the family stability by doing what you can to make it a stronger unit.

Fear for personal future: You'll never worry about this if you feel good about yourself. You might plan for your future. You might dream about what you would like to do, but you don't waste time worrying or being full of fear. It is a wasted exercise.

Unwanted pregnancy: Respect yourself and other people too much to ever engage in premarital sex. Believe in God's rules and His law. Who cares what *Playboy, Penthouse,* or *Hustler* says or what the TV portrays? What the people in the movies do as a way of life doesn't matter at all. There is God's way, and every other way is not His way. Being different is okay, because you *are* different with the Lord living in your heart.

If God has blessed you by making you a high achiever, don't let the worries and frustrations of this world cause you to focus on your problems and not what He has given you. The specialness that allows you to achieve above what many of the rest of us can should be used for His glory and benefit.

Take a moment and open your Bible and read Philipians 4:4–9. Notice how Paul, who was in prison, taught how to be full of joy. He gives the key to getting away from worry: pray more. Imagine not having to worry about anything! It seems impossible, because most of us worry at school, when we work, about our relationships with others. In verse 7 Paul shares how to have real peace. It comes from knowing that God is in control and that because we have a relationship with Jesus Christ, our destiny is secure and our victory over sin is certain. Let these words fill your heart and help you focus on the good things. Never again point your thoughts at feelings of worthlessness. The reason is simple: You've got too much to live for.

The solution is simple: Focus on the problem solver (Jesus), not your problems!

21
Respect = Listening To

Whenever my parents and I talk, we always end up shouting and yelling at one another. As a little boy once said, "Daddy, while I'm talking, I can't hear what you're saying." How can I respect my parents and why should I listen to them when they don't know anything that goes on in my generation or what's happening in this world? I tell them about things that happen at school, a movie, or a song, and they act like I'm from outer space. You keep mentioning respect, but how do I do it?

Respect means "listening to." When you respect your parents and they share something with you (even if they seem behind the times by about 4 million light years), you still need to listen to them, because wisdom comes with years. If you don't listen to them, you will miss out on some free wisdom. Doing what you want in this world will never get you ahead, but doing what you should do and what is right both get you ahead and keep you there. For instance, remember Job, who was down and out, afflicted with pain, had lost his family and possessions, and was covered from head to foot with boils and scars? All this happened so God could show Satan that some people won't curse God, no matter what. Three of Job's friends came to give him advice. They had talked to him for a long time. Each one gave advice that came strictly from left field: It was all wrong. All three supposed this and challenged Job to do that, and wondered this and that. A young man named Elihu listened to them and became upset, because he knew the instruction they were giving Job went against what was right. He got irritated.

Job 32:5: But when he [Elihu] saw that the three men had nothing more to say, his anger was aroused.

He knew that they were wrong and that their word carried no substance, but he didn't shout, and he didn't yell. Why did this young man not yell at these older men or argue with them, even though he knew that they were giving wrong information? The next two verses, Job 32: 6, 7, tell us why: "So Elihu son of Barakel the Buzite said: 'I am young in years, and you are old; that is why I was fearful, not daring to tell you what I know. I thought, "Age should speak; advanced years should teach wisdom."'"

I really don't know what happened to Elihu the rest of his life, but I know that God allowed this to happen and recorded it so you would have an example of a young person who confronted people who were older and wiser than he. Even though they may not know the exact facts at that moment, God's law still says that if you listen to older people, you will be better off. Your parents are older than you, and along with years comes wisdom. Listen to them. It just takes a little patience on your part, and it could have a lifelong effect on your happiness, respect, and friendship with them.

22
Prove It

Everybody wants us to prove something. Boyfriends tell girl friends, "If you love me, you'll go all the way. Prove your love for me by having sex today." Gang members are constantly asked to prove their loyalty, causing crime, rebelliousness, and even murder. Prove it! If you are loyal, kill or steal for the gang.

A friend of mine, Clebe McClary, had friendship proved to him once. He was in Vietnam and a hand grenade landed just a couple feet from him. A seventeen-year-old jumped on the hand grenade and gave up his own life so Clebe would not suffer. That is what I call really proving it.

"Prove it" is the same as "acting on it," but, *what actions*? Sex isn't the same as love. Stealing for someone isn't the same as being loyal. Killing someone isn't proving that you are a part of the team, even if your team is into drugs and murder.

We've got a great example in a woman who proved her love for her best friend—Jesus. Her name was Mary of Bethany. The Bible makes it clear the disciples did not understand Jesus when He said that He was going to suffer, die, and rise again on the third day.

Matthew 16:21, 22: From that time on Jesus began to explain to his disciples that he must go to Jerusalem and suffer many things at the hands of the elders, chief priests and teachers of the law, and that he must be killed and on the third day be raised to life.

Peter took him aside and began to rebuke him. "Never, Lord!" he said. "This shall never happen to you!"

Only Mary of Bethany understood. She did something to prove it, too: She acted on her belief. In those days, when people were buried, they were wrapped in linen clothes with spices in between the layers. To show that she knew He was going to rise again and wouldn't need those spices to be buried with, Mary put expensive perfume on Jesus when He was still alive. The disciples did not understand, because their faith was not that deep. Judas even condemned it because he thought she was wasting her money and that it should be given to the poor (John 12:4).

How have you proven your love lately for Jesus? Are you too busy to find creative ways to worship Him? Is your money, your time, or your strength too important to be poured out to Jesus today? Don't say you would die for him. Instead, He wants you to live for Him. Give Him the things that are precious to you.

John 14:14–21: "You may ask me for anything in my name, and I will do it.

"If you love me, you will obey what I command. And I will ask the Father, and he will give you another Counselor to be with you forever—the Spirit of truth. The world cannot accept him, because it neither sees him nor knows him. But you know him, for he lives with you and will be in you. I will not leave you as orphans; I will come to you. Before long, the world will not see me anymore, but you will see me. Because I live, you also will live. On that day you will realize that I am in my Father, and you are in me, and I am in you. Whoever has my commands and obeys them, he is the one who loves me. He who loves me will be loved by my Father, and I too will love him and show myself to him."

23
Half a Mustache

Dear Bill: No one ever notices me. My parents never brag about me or notice the good things that I do, like my brothers and sisters. Even at school it is as if people don't even know I'm alive.

Not to be noticed is a very hurting thing. It cuts deep. Often other people seem so busy, happy, and active, and we walk around hoping beyond hope that someone will notice. We say to ourselves, *Why can't someone see that I'm hurting? Oh, just to have one friend.* Or, *It would mean a lot to me to be able to share with someone who really cared!* We have all had times in our lives when we have felt obscure, lost in the crowd, and unnoticed.

With my brother, I visited an old friend in Florida. We were on the roof of his trailer, putting on a new coat of silver roofing compound, to protect it from the sun and keep it from leaking. At the time I had a mustache. For quite a while I had thought about shaving my mustache off, and right in the middle of that project I went down to get three tall glasses of iced tea. Just before I took them up to my brother and our friend on the roof, I went into the bathroom and shaved off half my mustache. I'll never forget it. It was all I could do to keep back my laughter and grin. I went up on the roof, gave them their glasses of iced tea, and we drank half of them, then set them down and went back to work. Inside I was splitting a gut. I was cracking up and trying as hard as I could not to laugh out loud. An hour and a half or two hours later, we finished the project and were ready to head down. As we climbed down, all of a sudden my brother said. "Look at Bill! He's only got half a mustache." I started laughing, and so did they. I told them that I had worked side by side with them for a couple of hours and they had never noticed.

To me that shows that quite often people don't mean any harm when they don't seem to notice or mention the things we've accomplished, tell us how proud they are of us, or even to say, "I care about you," "I'm glad to be your friend," or, "I love you," on a regular basis. Time is one of those things that each of us seems never to have enough of. Activities come by the dozens. We all have millions of things to do, and every time you turn around, someone wants you to do something else. Each of us must realize that with all we have to do, it takes just a little extra effort to notice someone.

Sometimes we are guilty of not noticing our friends or the accomplishments of loved ones, until we are shocked with something unbelievable that they have done—or even with a tragedy. It reminds me of what happened to Thomas. Not until he noticed and saw for himself that Christ had holes in His hands and feet would he have faith and actually believe.

Don't let today's business or tomorrow's activities rob you of faith, not only in God, but also in people. Faith says, "Though I don't hear you say you love me, I still trust that you do. And though I don't hear you or feel your pat on the back, I still feel good about myself and our relationship." Don't be in such desperate need for people to notice you that you don't like yourself if they don't.

John 20:29: "Because you have seen me, you have believed; blessed are those who have not seen and yet have believed."

24
I'll Take Care of You

He was about twenty years old, with a worried look on his face and tattoos on his arm. As I left the assembly early that morning, this young man who looked too old to be in high school said, "I need to talk to you. When can we talk? Please . . . I need some help."

I was being rushed from the high school to the junior high a few miles away, so I said, "Can we meet at lunch?"

"Okay, I'll try."

I didn't see him until that evening, before I spoke to the parents, when I saw him waiting for me. We didn't have time to talk beforehand, but he promised to be there afterwards. We both anxiously waited: me to help, and him to learn. From the look on his face, I knew he didn't want to talk to me about how he planned to face his bright future.

After the evening session I was signing autographs in my

books and telling people what the tapes contained, and so on. When I had gotten only about halfway done with the books and tapes, he appeared. "Let's talk now. We have a few moments," I invited him.

We sat down at a table, and before I knew it he unfolded his story. He was about to go into the army, and his future didn't seem bright. He had very little to live for. Did he know what it meant to have total peace in his heart and to know where he was going, why he lived, and what he was all about? I asked. He said, "No," then wondered, "What do you have that I don't have?" Whenever I hear that question, I know people need more than just positive thinking, more than just a few clichés, fancy words, or charming sentences. I knew he needed truth; he needed what gives me the hope of a lifetime, courage to handle each new day. He needed to have in his heart what I had in mine.

I shared the gospel with him: how Jesus died for us, rose again, loved us so much that He gave up His own life so we could have eternal life, died, was buried, went into hell and rose again so we would never have to go to hell. He paid the price for us! We must be sorry, I told him, and ask God to be our Lord and Savior and try to truly live for Him. That young man understood it all. He had been ready for a long time. I am sure other people had shared with him, because that evening, while we sat at the table, it was as though a glass jar had been placed around us. He prayed with me and asked Christ to come into his heart. He cried for his sins, he hurt, and I knew it was genuine. Within the next few minutes, we hugged and laughed together. I shared how he would be spending eternity with me in heaven someday. I got his address and I was going to send him some more materials. When we looked up, we realized we were alone in the entire cafeteria. Because people had sensed we had a special moment going, they gave us the freedom and space to share. The principal or superintendent (I can't remember which) came over to me and said, "That was a wonderful thing that you just did with that young man. I heard your conversation. I want you to know that we are going to keep the rest of these books and tapes for the school, and I will send you a check next week."

As I drove home, it was as though God was saying, "If you take care of My business, I will take care of you and your business." Because I stood up for God and was more interested in having a new Christian brother that evening than selling all the books and tapes in the world, I knew the joy of seeing another person come to the Lord. (That is the only time, by the way, that the angels jump in heaven and sing and shout—when a new Christian is born—when a sinner turns from Satan to the Lord.)

I have also seen that money, fame and popularity mean nothing when you are home alone at night, when you hurt inside because you have tried to keep a step ahead of everyone else and to be a big shot—and you've failed. I am just thankful that God touched my heart and wanted me to have another brother in heaven.

If you stand up for God, He will take care of you. If you memorize Scripture, he will make it easier for you to memorize your homework and your studies. Share Christ with a hurting person in school or at your job. God will give you a piece of happiness you can't describe any other way—you can't pay for it, you can't buy it, you can't find it—only God has it, and it is free. He wants to give it to you today. Let Him take care of you as He did me that wonderful night. If you haven't received this free gift from God—take it! If you've already "taken it," then "pass it along"!

Matthew 6:33: "But seek first his kingdom and his righteousness, and all these things will be given to you as well."

Matthew 10:32, 33: "Whoever acknowledges me before men, I will also acknowledge him before my Father in heaven. But whoever disowns me before men, I will disown him before my Father in heaven."

25
Powerful Imagination

Denis Waitley, author of *Psychology of Winning*, one of the all-time best-selling motivational cassette programs, is a friend of mine. One of his proudest accomplishments was working with returning Vietnam POWs, helping them make the transition from war to peace, from Vietnam to America, from hate to love.

Denis tells many stories about the power of imagination. One man was in prison for seven years. To keep from going crazy, he would play golf every day in his little cell. He would play eighteen holes, remembering all the courses he had ever played. He would go through each and every stroke, visualizing putting the tee in the ground, putting the ball on the tee, the exact brand name of the ball, and so on. He would look out over the beautiful fairway on the first hole; it was a par 4, 433 yard dogleg to the left. There were four sand traps, a little bit of water on the right side, and a very difficult hole—but he could do it. His drive went long and straight, 195 yards; then it hit and rolled another 15. His next shot was a long 3-iron. He played it just perfectly. He got his stance, his follow-through was absolutely gorgeous, the ball lifted up and went far and high, and it lay down on the green and sat there like a feather. Next the putt. He lined it up from three different ways. He checked it all—the wind, the green, the direction of the grass from the way it was mowed, and now his stroke. He didn't want to be short hunting this first birdie. All of a sudden he stroked the ball smooth and straight. Clunk! Right on the bottom.

Each day, each hole, each golf course, this prisoner of war would visualize them. Guess what? He came out of prison and played a fantastic round, without very much practice at all.

Another man Denis tells about saved his sanity by pretending he had a motorcycle. Every day he made the noise of a loud motorcycle in his cell. *Today I am going to go down to the beach, so here we go. Vrooom! Vrooom!* By the hour he would run that motorcycle, because he enjoyed doing it before the war, and that kept him going during the war.

The mind is very powerful. We have to keep it full of things that will keep us from dwelling on our problems. I have heard about other people in Vietnam (and other wars) who longed for God's Word in prison but could not obtain it. Many stories tell of Vietnam veterans who would write down the little bits of verses that they could remember on small sheets of paper, keep them hidden from the enemy, and this was their strength day in and day out. It reminds me of David in the Old Testament. He loved God's Word above everything.

In Psalms 119:127 he declared, ". . . I love your commands more than gold, more than pure gold."

Today's devotion ends with eight verses from Psalm 119. See if your desire for God's Word is as strong as David's. Focusing on these verses will give you the right image of God and His way of doing things, so you can handle any thought, challenge, or temptation that comes your way.

Psalms 119:121–128: I have done what is righteous and just; do not leave me to my oppressors. Ensure your servant's well-being;

let not the arrogant oppress me. My eyes fail, looking for your salvation, looking for your righteous promise. Deal with your servant according to your love and teach me your decrees. I am your servant; give me discernment that I may understand your statutes. It is time for you to act, O Lord; your law is being broken. Because I love your commands more than gold, more than pure gold, and because I consider all your precepts right, I hate every wrong path.

26
Let's Party!

Do you remember Len Bias, the great basketball star from Maryland? He was signed as the number-two draft pick with the Boston Celtics, and he was going to play under the most valuable player that year, Larry Bird. He had just received a million-dollar bonus for signing with a shoe company, but the night that happened, he died of an overdose of cocaine.

I've read a lot that has been written about Len Bias, and even though I've never met him, I miss him dearly. I love the game of basketball, and I wanted to see him perform his marvels on the parquet floor of the Boston Gardens, even though I'm a Detroit Pistons' fan. I will never see him, and neither will you. It all has to do with two words, the words Len Bias said as he left for the evening—let's party! Most teenagers all across America shout the same words every Friday and Saturday night.

The sad thing about Len Bias is also sad about many of our American young people. They are not creative enough to find new and different ways to enjoy life, to get high on life, to enjoy other's company or to have a laugh without being stoned or drunk. The night Len Bias died, he first drank alcohol, then hard liquor, then smoked a few marijuana joints, and ultimately took cocaine. In my opinion the cocaine did not really kill Len Bias—his inability to do something different, to go away from the crowd and to find a new and different way of saying "Yes" to life and his God-given talents, caused his death. He went along with the crowd, as most young people do every weekend.

I ask teenagers, "Why do you go to parties and drink and smoke?" Most say that it gives them something to do with their hands. I say, "So does picking your nose." Many young people wish they didn't have the pressures of alcohol, tobacco, or drugs around during the parties, but they seldom do anything about it. Len Bias had a friend who supplied him with drugs. With all of Len's talents, he had not the foresight or the wisdom to tell this jerk to get lost. He went along with someone who said he was his friend.

But no friend allows someone to sell drugs in the same bus or hallway. No friend allows the guy in the locker next to yours to have a drinking problem and never says anything. No friend walks by when someone is being put down in the cafeteria or being made fun of in front of the school. Friends don't allow a classmate to ridicule someone behind his back, nor do they let an audience in the auditorium be loud while the speaker tries to entertain or educate the student body. Friends never say, "Let's party" with the idea of drinking and using drugs. Please, the next time you hear the words *let's party,* suggest a new and different way. Rent a racquetball court, play charades, make up your own TV game, go for a picnic in the rain, go look at the sunset by the beach and build sand castles until midnight, get a videocamera and make your own video, or whatever. All you have to do is think and be motivated in your heart to use your God-given talents.

I once heard this statement: "Something great is going to happen to you. Will you be around when it does?" Think about that. Many times your capacity to say no determines your capacity to say yes to greater things. Read Psalm 55.

Psalms 55:12, 13: If an enemy were insulting me, I could endure it; if a foe were raising himself against me, I could hide from him, But it is you, a man like myself, my companion, my close friend.

27
Why Am I Jealous?

The Compact Encyclopedia of Psychological Problems, by Clyde M. Narramore, defines jealousy as: "An attitude of envy or resentment toward a more successful rival. Feelings of jealousy are usually the result of frustration in attempts to achieve a desired object."

The author also describes several causes of jealousy that can help you analyze yourself or someone you know. Jealousy can result from:

1. *The way your parents handled early relationships in your childhood.* If your parents compared you, or put you down, or made it obvious that you did not do as well as your brother or sister, this could have caused jealousy that can linger on for many years.

2. *The coming of a brother or sister.* When you were younger and a new baby brother or sister came along, all of a sudden you were not number one. All the time in the world wasn't spent with you by your parents, and therefore you may have become very jealous.

3. *Excessive competition.* If your parents challenge you to do too much or to live up to their images, or be this or that on the court or the field, or get grades that would equal theirs, to become a doctor or whatever, this could also bring on some inside insecurities that result in jealousy.

4. *Parental favoritism.* If your parents play favorites, you may become jealous.

5. *Feelings of insecurity and inadequacy.* Quite often jealousy has to do with each one of us comparing ourselves with others. We wouldn't do that if we felt secure and adequate —if we felt we were okay as we were.

6. *A lack of spiritual development.* When a person's thoughts are not controlled by Christ, he tends to compare his situation to others. Then being envious or jealous is only a natural outcome.

Mark 7:21–23: "For from within, out of men's hearts, come evil thoughts, sexual immorality, theft, murder, adultery, greed, malice, deceit, lewdness, envy, slander, arrogance and folly. All these evils come from inside and make a man 'unclean.'"

Why should anyone who believes in Christ as Savior and who has the creator of the universe living in his heart be jealous of anyone else? Maybe from time to time he should feel sorry for others—sorry enough, that is, to help them. Maybe he admires someone and where he has gotten in life because of hard work, stick-to-it-iveness, the ability to care for others, and the ability to carry on a dream when impossible odds faced him. These are great things to try to emulate and pull into his own life, but he shouldn't waste time being jealous. You, too, have better things for your time and your life. Remember, from within out of the heart of men proceed these evil thoughts, and jealousy is one of them.

28
The Highs and the Lows

Different personalities act and react differently. Some people are steady, secure, easygoing, and sail pretty smoothly through life—not many highs and not many lows, but steady. Then there are those of us who are high one day and low the next. We can get real excited, and our enthusiasm reaches an all-time high, but the next day our despair and depression might put us in the deepest valley that we've ever seen. For no apparent reason, we might fall to the bottom. Then all of a sudden we are up on the top again. Up and down.

Recently I wrestled with one of my lows; for no apparent reason I felt deeply depressed, sorry for myself, and I wondered, *How am I going to get out of this?* And, *Why am I not any happier, and how come I feel so depressed, even though I'm blessed so greatly?* I pleaded with God, asking Him to help me. "If my faith is as strong as I know it is, how come I get down for no reason at all? And how come I pop back up—but sometimes it takes a day and sometimes it takes two or three?"

Through His Word, God showed me that I am like a giant oak tree. I am big (I've been walking with Him for about ten years now); I'm strong in my faith and fairly secure. But I keep getting weak moments—these lows and depressions. He showed me that for a tree to grow it must have a continual input of sun, water, and the right temperature and atmosphere. I needed to continually have the input of His Word, prayer, quiet time with Him, and fellowship with other believers. Instead I was depending on all of my past feedings. As a new Christian I had memorized great quantities of Scripture. For the first four or five years I was in the Word greatly, but for the last four or five years that has not been the case. It had become hit or miss. I would read the Word and then not do it for a few days. I would memorize a Scripture here and there and then not do it for a while. When He showed me that if I was close to Him, I would be strong, I felt as though the depression lifted right off me. I was sitting in the Cincinnati airport when all of this took place. Then I looked in my Bible. My friend Gary had challenged me to memorize a verse a week through 1988. The verse for that week was 2 Corinthians 12:9. I had not looked at it and had not begun to memorize it. I opened up the Bible and finally looked:

2 Corinthians 12:9:   But he said to me, "My grace is sufficient for you, for my power is made perfect in weakness." Therefore I will boast all the more gladly about my weaknesses, so that Christ's power may rest on me.

I understood why we get low in our Christian walk, because God's strength is made perfect when we are weak. Only when we are on our backs do we look straight up. As long as we run through life, successful, happy, powerful, and popular, we look straight ahead. We also think, as we look into a mirror, that we are the reflection as well as the cause of our success. We get proud and puffed up, so we forget to look at God and give Him the thanks, the praise, and the glory for what we are and who we are—and the happiness and peace we possess.

Paul tells us he had recently been to heaven, though before verse 9 he was not sure if it was his body or his spirit. He describes heaven as too wonderful to tell about. In the same breath he reported that he begged God three times to take away his problem, which he called his thorn in his flesh, but God wouldn't. I begged God to take away my depression, and for a while He wouldn't take it away. He wanted me to dig deeper and to find out the secret, which was to be rooted in Him, His Word, and His fellowship.

I called my friend Gary that night and told him the exciting news. He told me he had prayed for me for several hours that day, and part of his prayer was that I would open up the Bible and memorize the verse we were supposed to memorize that week. Prayer is no coincidence. God listening to our prayer is not a hit-or-miss situation: He does it every single time. He will also respond to every single prayer with the answer that is best for us.

The highs and the lows—God showed me that we can stay out of the lows if we just stay strong. He also showed me that we will all fall many times. By the way, that is what God is there for anyway—to pick us up.

29
I Need to Talk

An anonymous fifth grader wrote to his parents: "When you get mad, I feel you want to throw me out for good. I still love you, but sometimes I'm so afraid of you that I can never talk to you. . . ."

Why do so many young people have to grow up in fear and pain? I think it's because kids merely model their parents: Most child abusers were abused children; you have twice the chance of becoming an alcoholic if one of your parents was; if profanity is part of the parents' vocabulary, why would we be amazed when the child swears?

Let's go back to this little boy's fear. What a terrible handicap to look at life through—angry parents whom you are too afraid to talk to. That is real fear, and it must be dealt with. For many young people, this is real life as they live it every day. His parents need the love of Christ, and they need to realize that this child is no different from Jesus. The way we treat any of our brothers and sisters, especially our children, is the same as treating Christ that way.

Maybe you can't change the family relationships of many of your hurting friends, but you can look at the devastating effect infuriated pride has and avoid it in your family. Take a moment and read Matthew 2:16–18 and see the results of such anger.

Here are some more tips from the handbook on life:

Proverbs 15:1: A gentle answer turns away wrath, but a harsh word stirs up anger.

Proverbs 15:18: A hot-tempered man stirs up dissension, but a patient man calms a quarrel.

Proverbs 16:32: Better a patient man than a warrior [hero], a man who controls his temper [anger] than one who takes a city.

Proverbs 20:2: . . . He who angers him [the king] forfeits his life.

Proverbs 21:14: A gift given in secret [being kind to someone] soothes anger, but a bribe concealed in the cloak pacifies great wrath.

It looks as if God wants our patience, not our anger. In some small way, let's try it today! Put a fire out—don't ignite it.

30
His Duesenberg

One of the marvelous things about what I do is meeting new friends, and I just had the great pleasure of meeting a man who loves kids as much as anyone I know. All through the school of 440 high school kids, he travels before, during, and after classes. They come to him, call him, hug him, ask him questions, look to him for wisdom, and see if they can help do any special projects. It is truly amazing. He has only been at this school for a couple of years, and already the entire school feels, *We are together. We are a team.* Juniors and seniors don't go to parties, like those at all the other schools I go to. On weekends they do projects and fun, exciting activities that show creativity and concern for one another. They go tobogganing, have creative progressive dinners, play a lot of racquetball, plan and produce their own videos. I had such a wonderful time the other day at this school, I must share a story.

My new friend is Father Marty, the spiritual advisor for this small Catholic high school in northern Indiana. Father Marty is a marvel. From time to time he writes little articles in their newsletter for the parents and kids. One had to do with his love for cars. As long as he can remember, he has had a passion for classic, restored automobiles. He told about a car show he was at one day, and car after car had the type of beauty that only comes from painful hours of attention, work, and restoration. All of them were classics, and they shined with a glitter and a gleam that made their owners proud. All of a sudden he saw an old truck pulling a trailer. On that trailer was a burned-out, rusted frame of an old Duesenberg. What was this piece of junk doing among all of these classics? He couldn't help notice something else. While the car didn't shine, the smile on the face of the owner, driving the pickup certainly did. He drove that right in the midst of that parade, and his face clearly shouted to those watching, "This is my Duesenberg"! He felt so proud and looked from side to side. You could see that someday he was going to restore that old piece of tin into a marvel.

Father Marty also mentioned that it caused him to think of how God must see us. Before we turn to Him and become cleansed of our sins, in our state of despair, we must look like that pile of burnt-out, rusted junk. But God sees something that shines in us—the capacity to love and be loved. He saw it in us so long ago that before we were even born He sent His pride and joy to die on the cross for us.

Today we need to ask ourselves, *Where am I in this procession?* Are you looking battered and hurt, like a piece of junk? Is your life-style and the way you carry yourself and stay groomed like that old Duesenberg on the back end of that trailer, or are you becoming something God can smile about?

God is proud of us and loves us so very much. Are we letting Him down or living up to His expectations? Within each one of us is the ability to shine in God's procession that shows the world we are proud of our Lord and that He has done marvelous things with us.

Ephesians 2:10: For we are God's workmanship, created in Christ Jesus to do good works, which God prepared in advance for us to do.

I like the way *The Living Bible* phrases that verse, "It is God himself who has made us what we are and given us new lives from Christ Jesus; and long ages ago he planned that we should spend these lives in helping others." Our new lives are like that new, finely tuned, shined automobile —the Duesenberg. Realize, please, that you are a very beautifully created thing from God Almighty. Shine for the Lord today.

31

Save a Life . . . Stop a Suicide

If one of your friends threatened to commit suicide, would you act as if he'd made a joke? Would you laugh it off or would you know how to help her? Do you know what signs to look for? Don't just say that it only happens to other people. Today suicide is the second-biggest killer of young people between the ages of fifteen and twenty-four. Each one of us knows of a family in which a person has taken his or her own life.

According to the American Association of Suicidology, five distinct warning signs should automatically alert us to a potential suicide:

1. *A suicide threat or other statement indicating a desire or intention to die.* If you ever hear one of your friends say, "I can't take this pressure anymore," "Life isn't worth it," "The stress is too great," or, "I just can't take it," don't take these threats idly! Take them for real. Notice when your friend has his head slumped and is acting different—

79

especially standing by the locker, walking down the hall, or in the cafeteria.

2. *A previous suicide attempt.* I recently heard a woman tell about a student who tried to erase herself to death. That's right—rubbing an eraser on each wrist. No one noticed it in class. After she tried an eraser, rubbing it back and forth over and over again, she turned to a paper clip—rubbing it over and over on her skin. No one noticed, so she turned to glass and finally to a razor blade. Please keep your eye out for other kids and loved ones who have mentioned a previous suicide attempt or who are doing things indicating that.

3. *Mental depression.* There is a lot of stress for young people today—and for parents as well. Juniors and seniors constantly talk to me about the amount of stress, keeping their grades up, what school to go to, what to do after high school or college, how to put up with what everyone expects them to do, and so on. The only way to deal with this kind of stress is to develop coping skills. Talk to your friends. Pump iron or exercise. If you like to be alone, be alone, or if you like to be with other people, then be with them. If music helps you enjoy yourself and forget your pressures, then try it. Just remember—don't try to cope with depression through things that add to the depression. Alcohol and drugs only add to the long-term depression. Cope in a positive way.

4. *Marked changes in personality or behavior.* As a friend you will notice "mood swings" before anyone else. You are around that person more than anyone else, and you can tell when he or she changes.

5. *Making arrangements, as though for a final departure.* When other students start giving away things such as jewelry, pets, a record collection, and so on, *beware!* (Especially if that person is in a good mood.) If you've noticed that someone has been bummed out for two or three weeks and then becomes high, happy, smiling, and starts giving things away, this is a very important

warning sign—maybe the most important of all—for you to notice. Your friend seems happy because she has an inner peace; she has made the decision to kill herself. In her mind she thinks she's found the right answer.

What do you do if you recognize these signs in a friend? Follow these steps:

1. *Discuss the topic of suicide openly and frankly. Do not be afraid to use the word* suicide *in your discussion.* Remember, you are a friend and not a counselor, but you can help. Don't be fake, be genuine. Others have laughed at your friend and said, "You won't do it," "You'll never carry it through," or, "You're just talking about it." Don't make the same mistake!

2. *Show interest and support.* Be honest. Don't just try to get that person through the first hour, second hour, and third hour. Give him positive reinforcement. Let him know you really care. If you see he is doing something fantastic or positive, tell him about it. Be a genuine friend. Honesty and sincereness are vitally important here. If he doesn't see that you show interest and give support, he will probably feel you are just like his parents (who may be ignoring him and too busy for him) or like other friends who have not picked up on the signals. Please, be interested and show support. One of the best things you can say is, "I really care about you, and I want to do what I can to help," or, "You are my friend. I don't want to lose my friend. I want you here with me. I care about you, and I am going to be here to help . . . no matter what or how long it takes."

3. *Get professional help!* Tell somebody you believe can help, someone you can trust. *Don't* keep this a secret. You've got to get professional help: a teacher, a counselor, or an adult trained in this, who can talk to your friend. Even if your friend looks you in the eye and says, "I'll hate you the rest of my life, if you tell anyone," it doesn't matter. You must get professional help. Continually tell him you care, and

that is the reason you are doing this. I guarantee you that he will come back later—maybe many weeks or months later—and thank you for being there, holding strong, and doing what was right. He might feel angry and hate you, but keep telling him that you are doing it because you do care about him.

After one senior took his own life, others found out what had happened before the suicide. He told all eight of his friends how he was going to kill himself, when he was going to do it, and even why. All eight ignored it. They all tried to hide it, and each one told him to his face that he would not carry it out—but he did! Now they have lost a friend, and all of them feel angry with themselves and him, but they are also frustrated and very guilty. They will have to carry that scar for the rest of their lives.

People are too important and life is too precious for us to let caring go by the wayside, for us not to pick up warning signs and not have steps to follow when someone hurts. Encourage others to read this chapter, too, and know the signs.

Find the suicide crisis line in your area. You can call it anytime. Help someone who hurts. Most of all, *care*. Then know what to do. With God as your helper, you will have the strength to notice and follow through with the help that is needed to save a life.

When someone feels heavy under the burdens and pressures of stress, depression, or hopelessness, give him the ultimate gift: Jesus Christ. He makes a plea to your hurting friend and to you when you are down and out:

Matthew 11:28–30: "Come to me, all you who are weary and burdened, and I will give you rest. Take my yoke upon you and learn from me, for I am gentle and humble in heart, and you will find rest for your souls. For my yoke is easy and my burden is light."

32
Life Got Tough, but She Got Tougher

A beautiful girl taught me about being tough on the inside. Not fighting tough and not angry tough, but having toughness that comes from inner strength. I tell her story everywhere I go.

She is a neighbor of mine, Nikki. She came down with leukemia and lost all her hair. What she did one Monday morning before school started has changed many lives and given many of us hope to carry on no matter how difficult a situation is—how afraid we are of what lies ahead. She wore a wig, but got tired of it, so she took it off. In the backseat of the car that morning, as she took it off, she told her mom and dad, "Today I am going to find out who my real friends are." She walked across the schoolyard and into the school and received nothing but respect from her classmates. You see, life got tough when it dealt Nikki the hard blow of leukemia, followed by chemotherapy and many hours in hospitals. But Nikki got tougher.

Nikki would ask you, "What will have to happen to you in order for you to toughen up, to decide what is right and wrong for you, to say, 'I'm going to stand on my own two feet, on my own morals, on my own convictions, and I will never again be ashamed of my faith in God or my love for other people (enough love, that is, to never have them lose any respect for me or themselves). I will never do anything to compromise what I stand on.'" We find it easy to laugh at other people, but can we laugh at ourselves? That's tough. It is easy to sit by our friends at the game, but can we ask a kid who is new at school, unpopular, or just plain bad looking to join us and sit by us? That's tough! We can walk through the halls with our friends and snicker at other people whom we don't like or don't know, but can we leave our friends and walk over to another student who is all alone and ask him if he needs a friend? That's tough! Do we stop the fight, clean up the blackboard when we didn't mess it up, pick up paper we didn't drop, or turn a frown into a smile? That's tough!

Remember Nikki. Remember that when life gets tough, if you want to, God will help you toughen up on the inside and handle it. You can do it! Go make it happen.

Matthew 10:21–31: "Brother will betray brother to death, and a father his child; children will rebel against their parents and have them put to death. All men will hate you because of me, but he who stands firm to the end will be saved. When you are persecuted in one place, flee to another. I tell you the truth, you will not finish going through the cities of Israel before the Son of Man comes.

"A student is not above his teacher, nor a servant above his master. It is enough for the student to be like his teacher, and the servant like his master. If the head of the house has been called Beelzebub, how much more the members of his household!

"So do not be afraid of them. There is nothing concealed that will not be disclosed, or hidden that will not be made known. What I tell you in the dark, speak in the daylight; what is whispered in your ear, proclaim from the housetops. Do not be afraid of those who kill the body but cannot kill the soul. Rather, be afraid of the one who can destroy both soul and body in hell. Are not two sparrows sold for a penny? Yet not one of them will fall to the ground apart from the will of your Father. And even the very hairs of your head are all numbered. So don't be afraid; you are worth more than many sparrows."

Tough isn't being rough. It's being strong enough on the inside to act right on the outside.

33
Modern Love

I just saw a TV special hosted by Geraldo Rivera that has still got my mind spinning and my blood pressure just a bit high. When I turned it on, Reverend Jerry Falwell was talking with the publisher of *Penthouse* magazine. I didn't bother to remember or write down the publisher's name, as I don't care to have that item in my mind. My Bible challenges me in Romans to renew my mind with thoughts of good and beauty. This didn't seem to be one.

The publisher was saying that enough Americans want sex, whether it be over their dial-a-porn, or legalized prostitution in parts of Nevada, or reading and looking at his magazine, and there was nothing anyone could do about it. He said that when young people dial his phone number, where they can hear explicit sexual messages of XXXX- or XXXXX-rating caliber, it does them no harm at all. He said that until they get to the age where they are ready to engage in sex, these messages will have absolutely no meaning to them at all. I just about vomited as I was watching the TV. I felt proud of Jerry Falwell as he shared that many Christians in this country still believe in the beautiful way God has planned and prepared sex to remain in the confines of holy matrimony, where a husband and wife, who have been joined together in God's name, can share this beautiful experience.

The report went on to talk about AIDS, condoms, and several other topics that seem to be hot news. The only method they could come up with to prevent AIDS was to use condoms when having sex. Never once did they mention abstaining from sex before marriage. Never once did they mention anything about God's rule—and living in hurt anger, and frustration, when you break it. I get so many letters from girls who regret saying yes to boyfriends who begged them to prove their love that it tears my heart apart. Part of them was taken away—a part that will never be brought back again.

When you watch TV and come across a program like that or view sexual messages in advertising, soap operas, sit-coms, or award-winning shows, *think*. Use your brain as well as your eyes when you watch TV—they are meant to work together. Ask yourself who the producer is. *Does he have any spiritual foundation? Does he care what happens to me, what I think about, or how I act in my life? Do the writers of this material really care about me?* Remember this: When someone wants your money, they might do anything to get it, especially if they don't have a good Christian foundation. If someone sells you drugs or a drink, he doesn't care about you. He wants to make a buck, support his habit, or have someone else do what he is doing so he won't feel so bad.

When a beer company states that they care about us and that is why they want us to drink only what we can handle, I can hardly stand it. When cigarette commercials say, "If you must smoke, smoke my brand," it really shows me how much they care.

Look around yourself today and see who really wants your attention, wants you to make him feel good, wants your money, wants you to buy his product, or whatever. Look at their true motives. You will come back to some very special people in your life who only want the best for you: your God, your parents, your special friends and teachers, the special people in your life whom you can talk with and who spend hour after hour trying to reach you (like your youth pastor or your counselor at school). Just because something is modern—even love—doesn't mean that it is right. It also doesn't mean that it is going to help you at all in the long run. Make the right choice.

1 Thessalonians 5:21, 22: Test everything. Hold on to the good. Avoid every kind of evil.

34
Revenge of the Nerds

Revenge! Get even! They've got it coming! They made me look bad! Do any of these sound familiar? Each year thousands of people, young and old, ruin their lives forever because they are nerds: They live and act on revenge.

I wasted my entire eleventh grade in high school wanting to get even with a fellow who embarrassed me in front of the entire student body. Over and over revenge caused me to visualize getting even. I harbored it.

Revenge has recently caused a fired airline worker to take a gun on a flight and kill his ex-boss, as well as the pilot, causing everyone on the plane to die.

What does God's Word say about anger? Should we ever be angry? Go to God's "blueprint for life" (His Word), and you will once again see that every problem we will ever encounter is answered plainly for our immediate use. Look at Luke 3:19, 20 and find out why Herodias was angry at John the Baptist. Was she embarrassed in public? Did she forgive him or let her revenge brew like a hot pot of coffee? Now look at the results of revenge when it isn't left to God or when we don't make up with the other person. Read Mark 6:17–29, and dig out these interesting facts from the verses: (1) Did you see how Herod was affected by peer pressure? (2) See how he was embarrassed to do what he knew was right.

Now look at God's rule concerning anger. Read Ephesians 4:26. God doesn't tell us we should never be angry. Sin and Satan are to be hated, but we must deal with our anger immediately so we do not lose relationships for a lifetime.

Ephesians 4:26: . . . Do not let the sun go down while you are still angry.

Have you ever noticed how hard it is to sleep if you haven't made up with your parents or friend? This one rule could save many relationships and marriages. Don't be a nerd! Get rid of revenge!

35
Hurts on the Inside

Dear Bill: When I grew up I was sexually abused by my brother. It lasted for several years, and no one knew anything about it. That's a long time ago, and I am a Christian now, but I still feel much pain and guilt inside. Please help! Your friend, Hurting.

Dear Hurting: I am so sorry that you had to experience such an ongoing nightmare. Child abuse and abuse of any kind, whether sexual, physical, mental, or emotional, leave scars that last for a long time. There are some helpful steps that I would like to share with you:

1. You need to realize that it was *not* your fault. You were the victim.
2. Bathe yourself in God's Word and His love. Read the Bible. Find out just how much God loves you. Read accounts of how Jesus died on the cross, was beaten and spat upon, and how He must have hurt, as well.
3. Confess any known sin and accept God's forgiveness. Realize that He has certainly forgiven you for any part you think you might have played, especially since you were just the victim. Whether or not you caused it to happen,

God's forgiveness is complete. Read 1 John 1:9 and realize that He forgives all our confessed sins.

4. Forgive your brother (Matthew 6:14). Many times people harbor guilt, pain, shame, and hurt from the past because anger won't let it escape. If that is the case with you, go to a quiet place, turn it over to God, and truly tell God you forgive your brother. I might add that most likely your brother has also been hurting deeply all these years. He doesn't want to bring it up, and he is afraid to see you or talk about it. Many times brothers and sisters with situations like this never see each other for years and years; if they get together for Christmas, they sit quietly and never go in the same room or talk. The pain just lingers.

5. Try to go to your brother and tell him you forgive him. You don't need to mention any details; he will know what you are talking about. Just say, "When we were growing up, many of the things that happened . . . well, I have forgiven you for all of them." This will make you the bigger person and really put you in harmony with God's way of restoring relationships, feelings, and self-dignity (Matthew 5:41).

6. Talk it out! Seek a good biblical counselor. Find a counselor who believes that the final authority of everything we deal with must be God's Word. Bring your pain, hurt, and anger out in the open. Many times your counselor will want you to share what actually happened so you can get it out and deal with it. Check out your counselor very closely before meeting, but once you find one whom you can trust, make sure you go for at least four or five sessions. If your pain still lingers, there are group sessions where you can share with people, to hear about their victories.

7. Ask for forgiveness from anyone you have hurt. Quite often sin leads to more sin. People who are abused sometimes abuse others, get involved with premarital sex, or have affairs outside marriage. Whatever it may have been, seek God's forgiveness. If your sin did not take place too long ago, go to the person and seek forgiveness as well. If that person is married and has a family, then drop it. If you

dated years ago and can't locate someone, then forget it. Don't let anyone tell you that because you didn't meet with a person, the sin remains and forgiveness will not take place. God does not want you to startle an entire family or to break a relationship between that person, a spouse, or family members. God wants you to come to Him and let Him cleanse you.

As you read this, maybe you're thinking, *I've never been abused sexually.* But someone near you (either in your family, your class, your school, or where you work) probably has been treated unfairly in the past, abused, and harbors much guilt. Loan this book to that person so he or she can read the steps that will bring a peaceful life. I would also encourage you to help that person focus on the fact that Jesus knows what it is to hurt, feel pain, and have anger, fear, and frustration.

When Jesus was in the Garden of Gethsemane, He was afraid. He knew that in a little while God the Father would totally abandon Him. He would have to enter hell itself, in order to take our place there. He didn't concentrate on rising from the dead, but He hurt, because He saw what lay right in front of Him. Notice what He did to eliminate his fears and inner hurt: He chose to do God's will. The steps I have given you are not easy and not popular, but they are God's way.

God's way—forgiveness, moving forward, forgetting, and getting help—is not what the world has taught us to do, feel, and act on in situations like these. The world would have us be angry and get even. Like David, in the Old Testament, do you have a Goliath (a giant) in your life? With God's help and your hand on the slingshot, you, too, can kill that emotional monster in your life. (Read 1 Samuel 17.)

1 Samuel 17:49:   Reaching into his bag and taking out a stone, he slung it and struck the Philistine on the forehead. The stone sank into his forehead, and he fell facedown on the ground.

36
Who to Cling To

Elton John sings the popular song about Marilyn Monroe, "Candle in the Wind." There is a phrase in there that could be said of many of us: It talks about never knowing what to hang on to when life gets real tough. Each one of us has to ask that question. When the things go wrong (life's troubles, depressions, worries, problems, and so on), what and who do I cling to?

I've known people who have gathered friends about them, and as long as people surrounded them, they seemed happy. But they couldn't stand being alone. Many people feel frightened to be alone because they have never grown to know themselves. Many people become workaholics because that seems to provide security, and it keeps their minds off life's troubles or the challenges they should concentrate on.

I have witnessed many parents moving farther and farther from their children because they just couldn't understand their teens' problems. I've read of many parents who, because of a handicap of one sort or another in a child or mate, have left, never to be seen again or heard of. When the rain sets in, who do you hold on to?

Whenever I'm on a speaking engagement I never ignore

one important thing: I always make sure people know that I am confident, can carry myself the way I do, can handle life and whatever it throws at me because of who I cling to. I cling to the rock, not merely sand. Jesus is the rock of ages. He is the only person never to have done wrong, lie, or mislead anyone. He has never done anything for selfish gain or to hurt anyone. His goal is that each one of us might live—really live. He has given us a book in which we can find every answer to every problem. Any kind of rain, problem, or storm that comes toward us is answered in His book.

Elton John said he wished he could have known Marilyn Monroe. I wish Marilyn and Elton could both know the person of Jesus Christ, my strength. When you lean on Christ (the rock), it's amazing: Rains, as they come, do not have scary thunderbolts, and the winds never blow you over.

The next time you hear that song, ask yourself, *Who am I leaning on? Who am I clinging to at this moment?* If you're sinking, you're not standing on the right thing. Your body won't budge on the solid rock. Read Matthew 7:24–27.

Matthew 7:24:   "Therefore everyone who hears these words of mine and puts them into practice is like a wise man who built his house on the rock."

Matthew 8:25–27:   The disciples went and woke him, saying, "Lord, save us! We're going to drown!"

He replied, "You of little faith, why are you so afraid?" Then he got up and rebuked the winds and the waves, and it was completely calm.

The men were amazed and asked, "What kind of man is this? Even the winds and the waves obey him!"

Psalms 119:169-176:   May my cry come before you, O Lord; give me understanding according to your word. May my supplication come before you; deliver me according to your promise. May my lips overflow with praise, for you teach me your decrees. May my tongue sing of your word, for all your commands are righteous. May your hand be ready to help me, for I have chosen your precepts. I long for your salvation, O Lord, and your law is my delight. Let me live that I may praise you, and may your laws sustain me. I have strayed like a lost sheep. Seek your servant, for I have not forgotten your commandments.

37
Am I a Counterfeit?

Bank tellers almost never see counterfeit bills. However, when they come across one, they instantly know it—not because they have studied fake bills, but because they know what the real thing looks like. They know that by comparison, this is not real—it is a phony. For most of us it's different in real life: We see phonies so much that we don't know what the real thing is.

For instance, most people do not know what real love is. They confuse it with sex, romance, or lust, because they never see the real thing. In the realm of integrity, most people only see hypocrites. From evangelism to politics, from Wall Street to our own backyards, people say one thing, but lie and cheat on the sly.

What about families that are forever? Very few of us see those. We see abuse and divorce, but not commitment for a lifetime. How about true friends? Most of us don't know what one is. We know friends that are too busy to call, never there when we need them, who like to talk behind our backs, and so on.

One character who hung around with Jesus was a counterfeit. In fact, many people call him the most tragic figure in all history. His name was Judas. He lived with Jesus, he saw the miracles, he heard firsthand that Jesus said He was the Son of God, and he pretended to believe, but he never did. Though Judas could have believed and could have changed, he didn't. Instead he died a counterfeit.

Now ask yourself: *Am I a counterfeit? Do I pretend to believe? Am I a counterfeit when it comes to being a Christian; do I merely go to church and expect that by going over and over again I will become a Christian?* (Going into a doghouse does not make you a dog!) *Am I a counterfeit in my friendships? Do I lead someone on to believe that I am his best friend or a great friend and never invite him to the important things, never confide what is really on my heart, never ask how I can help him or pray for him and so on?* We can be counterfeits in many areas of our lives.

Judas saw Christ firsthand, but guess what? We have even more evidence on which to believe in Jesus than Judas did. We have His Word (much more in the Bible at our fingertips than Judas did, knowing Christ firsthand). We've got years' worth of archaeological discoveries to show us that what the Bible says is true. We've got many people who can say that their lives changed and that God is still in the miracle business. Perhaps you can even say that yourself. But, "Just because we are close to the truth doesn't mean that we are dedicated to it." The truth is that Judas was close to Jesus, but he wasn't dedicated. He gave Him up and betrayed Him. He did it with what a friend would do—a kiss.

Don't be a counterfeit, and don't be a fake. Be real! Life is too special to waste away. Like the counterfeit bills in the bank, wet ink and fake paper may look good on the outside, but deep down, you're nothing more than a disgrace if you aren't for real.

Acts 1:16–20: "Brothers, the Scripture had to be fulfilled which the Holy Spirit spoke long ago through the mouth of David concerning Judas, who served as guide for those who arrested Jesus—he was one of our number and shared in this ministry."

(With the reward he got for his wickedness, Judas bought a field; there he fell headlong, his body burst open and all his intestines spilled out. Everyone in Jerusalem heard about this, so they called that field in their language Akeldama, that is, Field of Blood.)

"For," said Peter, "it is written in the book of Psalms, " 'May his place be deserted; let there be no one to dwell in it. . . .' "

38
Be Careful What You Study!

Across the country, we hear about teachers who have students do research on other religions besides Christianity. Students really get involved with one very scary religion, when they do research and study it. Usually, however, their study earns them an A, so many will dig deeper and learn more about it.

A fourteen-year-old young man in New Jersey did a paper on Hinduism. But he became more interested in this religion the other kids were doing—the one almost guaranteed to earn him an A—Satanism. School officials and his fellow students say this boy became defiant and hostile while burying himself in library books on the occult and listening to heavy-metal rock music. Teachers noticed the difference, and on a Thursday they warned his mother, but by Saturday night both mother and the son were dead. The son said he had a vision in which Satan came to him, wearing his own face, and urged him to kill his family. He preached Satanism. The boy stabbed his mother at least twelve times, and tried to kill his father and ten-year-old brother by setting fire to the house. Then he slit his own throat and wrist with a Boy Scout knife—and died in a pool of blood on the snow in a neighbor's backyard.

It is very dangerous to mess with the occult. For several years now I have spoken against the popular game Dungeons and Dragons, that gets participants to look deeper into the occult, to learn chants as well as other ways to get in touch with Satanic spirits. I urge you to get rid of any Ouija boards you or your friends have. Never mess with anything occult. If you listen to a band who prays to Satan, get rid of their albums. If you know any kids in school who play Dungeons and Dragons, get them help immediately by notifying someone who cares. You may save their lives.

The Bible instructs us to be naive in the things of the world, but Satan wants each one of us to commit suicide. He encourages us to make ourselves bigger than God.

Look at Isaiah 14:11–14, which describes Satan's fall:

All your pomp has been brought down to the grave, along with the noise of your harps; maggots are spread out beneath you and worms cover you. How you have fallen from heaven, O morning star, son of the dawn! You have been cast down to the earth, you who once laid low the nations! You said in your heart, "I will ascend to heaven; I will raise my throne above the stars of God; I will sit enthroned on the mount of assembly, on the utmost heights of the sacred mountain. I will ascend above the tops of the clouds; I will make myself like the Most High."

Notice how Satan uses the word *I*. He says, "*I* will ascend to heaven. *I* will raise *my* throne above the stars. *I* will sit on the mount. *I* will ascend above the heights. I will make myself like the Most High." Satan's entire game plan is to make us think someone could be greater than God, as when he was called in verse 12 "morning star." He tried to become greater than God, but he was cast out of heaven and into the pits of hell. When we mess with him, study him, and deal with anything that has to do with him—fortune-tellers, tarot cards, or anything that has to do with Satanism and the occult—that happens to us, too. It is very dangerous.

Whenever Satan challenges us, we can quote the words of Jesus in His confrontation with the devil:

Matthew 16:23: Jesus turned and said to Peter, "Out of my sight, Satan! You are a stumbling block to me; you do not have in mind the things of God, but the things of men."

Once again we can take the answer from God's book, when it comes to getting rid of Satan. James 4:7 says, "Submit yourselves, then, to God. Resist the devil, and he will flee from you." Hear the power in God's Word. The devil won't walk slowly away from you if you give yourself humbly to God; he will flee from you. *Flee* means "to run rapidly." Just say, in faith, "In the name of Jesus Christ, I command you, Satan, to be gone."

39
Why Don't They Care?

Whenever I ask my parents if I can do something or go somewhere, they always say "go ahead." They never care what I do. Many of my friends are jealous of my situation, but I don't like it. Can you help me?

Total freedom is a very scary thing, so God gave us rules and regulations. If you drove across a bridge, you would want guard rails on both sides of the bridge, because they give you a sense of security. Kids on playgrounds feel more secure knowing that there is a fence around the playground, but the grass always looks greener on the other side of the fence.

If we have parents who give us rules and regulations, we get jealous and envy those who don't. But teens who don't have any guidelines from their parents know that it's not all it's cracked up to be. They wish Mom and Dad would say no once in a while, and that they didn't have to make every decision on their own.

If your parents don't say no, I know how you must feel. I suggest that you talk to them and tell them you need their guidance and want their opinions on things to do and things not to do.

Ask your parents what rules and regulations they grew up with, how they appreciated them, and which ones they broke or wish they hadn't. Ask them if they thought their parents were too lenient or too strict. I think you will find that your parents are, for the most part, doing the best that they can. Remember, your parents were not trained to be parents. They had a child, so they became parents. You were never really trained to be a teenager. You turned thirteen. Together the two of you have got to work this out. One day soon, you'll be on your own. That is why, in many of these situations, I ask you to go to and to help your parents. Come up with a solution both of you can live with. I hope your solution will not break God's rule, but will encourage you to grow closer to God, so you can each feel good about yourselves and live up to your true potential.

Whenever I mention to kids that they are blessed when their parents have the courage to say no, they always snicker and wish their parents would give them more freedom. But the letter I started with shows how easily that can become just as damaging as a too-structured reationship. Talk to your mom and dad and try to work this out.

Proverbs 19:20, 21: Listen to advice and accept instruction, and in the end you will be wise. Many are the plans in a man's heart, but it is the Lord's purpose that prevails.

40
Delayed Flight

Since I spend so much time flying, I have a great opportunity to see many types of people, in airports and on airplanes and waiting in line for baggage that doesn't arrive. We have to joke about it, because if we couldn't, we'd never be able to make it. If you can't laugh at lost luggage and delayed flights and you fly a lot, you will go crazy. Whenever the flight gets delayed, I see three types of people:

One group gripes, complains, yells, and goes almost insane for the entire time the plane is delayed. Such people go to the counter and yell at the girl, who has nothing to do with the plane being on the ground. They tell her she has ruined their day, and she will never see them here again. She probably doesn't want to see them again. Many of them get upset because the plane cannot fly with only one engine. It's as if they say, "Make it fly. We can make it." Those are the gripers. We have them in all areas of life.

The second group heads straight for the bar. They drink for the three or four hours that the plane is delayed. Many people in life, as well, use all kinds of outside resources, liquids, and chemicals to help forget their troubles.

The people in the third group pick up a good book or do their work. They realize that they have a special opportunity to have some quiet time alone to read or get extra work done —uninterrupted, no kids, no noises at home, no phone calls, and no meetings to make.

When they finally call the plane, the same three groups get on. The gripers are still griping. Their entire day was ruined. The second group, those in the bar, could care less how late the plane was. Many times they are not sure how long the delay really was, because of their present situation and state of mind. The third group accomplished something, had some special quiet time by themselves, looked at it as a blessing and not a problem, and went home with blood pressure still intact, not worrying about hangovers or headaches later that evening.

Are you a bad-mouther, a bar hopper, or a book reader? The choice is yours. Remember, you can plan your actions, but you can never plan your reactions ahead of time. The way you react to situations out of your control shows more about your personality than all of your planned actions put together.

A long time ago, in the Old Testament, Joshua challenged the entire nation of Israel about choices. What gods were they going to follow? Were they going after the idols or the true and living God? You and I face the same choices today. Will popularity, drugs and alcohol, or having sex at any cost be your god? Or will you follow what Joshua said? Your destination—where you end up—is a lot more serious than lost luggage or delayed flights!

Joshua 24:15: "But if serving the Lord seems undesirable to you, then choose for yourselves this day whom you will serve, whether the gods your forefathers served beyond the River, or the gods of the Amorites, in whose land you are living. But as for me and my household, we will serve the Lord."

41

Psalm 1

Before you read today's message, please open your Bible and read through Psalm 1. There are only six verses, but they show you, in beautiful, poetic language, the contrast between two life-styles, as well as two very different destinies we can choose forever and ever. Verse one shares how you can be blessed. If you do not do certain things, God will bless you. Don't walk in the counsel of the wicked, it says. This means don't learn from people who don't love the Lord. Don't listen to their advice. Don't ask for their suggestions. Don't be impressed with their opinions.

God's Word also says not to "stand in the way of sinners or sit in the seat of mockers." The word *sinner* here implies a person who habitually sins, who loves evil rather than good, who would rather make Satan happy than God. Don't hang around such people or be their friends and continually be seen with them.

You might say to yourself that Jesus was the friend of sinners, but look what He did when He was in their company. He broke bread. He was with them, but He was there to teach them about the right way. He didn't hang around somebody for four or five years, never pretending or letting him know where He stood spiritually and morally.

He told them right up front. He was there to teach them. He did it tactfully, and He didn't offend them, but He did challenge them. Quite often people followed Him and accepted Him, or they didn't. When we hang around people who do us no good and who we deep down inside know don't care for God and His ways, we cop out. We will not be blessed.

Verse 2 says that real blessings come to a person who delights in the law of the Lord. Meditate on it day and night. Don't sit around with your hand under your chin, thinking, but constantly mull over God's Word and His commandments in your mind. Whenever you do something during the day ask yourself, Would this please God? As you begin to think about an activity, a statement, or a sentence, because God's Word is on your heart you should say to yourself, Should I or shouldn't I? Whenever God is on your heart and in your mind the answer is easy. You don't have to think twice or wonder is this right or is this wrong.

Be "like a tree planted by streams of water" (v.3). This means that you need not thirst, hurt on the inside, or be lonely or depressed. If you think on God's Word and do not hang around people who have made it obvious that they oppose the ways of our Lord, you will yield fruit in your season. Your leaf will not wither and you shall be successful and prosper, as it says in verse 3. When it talks about yielding fruit in its season, remember, a tree only has one season when it produces fruit, and as a believer you cannot expect only good to happen to you. A tree doesn't have fruit all year long, and neither do things continuously go well for Christians. Realize that there is a time and a place. Sometimes God does not allow wonderful things to happen to you, because you need to learn a lesson or receive a message He has shouted for some time, and He wants you to enjoy the blessing of something that maybe you can't handle at that time.

A great friend of mine, Zig Ziglar, shared with me that he never had wealth until he could handle it. Several times, before he became famous and successful financially, he had opportunity after opportunity to make large amounts of money, but he didn't because God knew that he couldn't handle it. God wants the best for us; He wants good things to happen to us when we can handle them and when we know what is best. Most of all, God wants our hearts. He knows that we love Him if we desire to do what His Word says, rather than be popular with people who don't like his Word. He knows where we stand, and He knows exactly how we feel on the inside.

Please God, and watch how the cool drops of water go through you just like that tree by the stream. Your leaf will not wither; I believe this means you will look young and happy. Have you ever noticed a person who feels anger or bitterness or has been sad or depressed for a while? It's hard for him to make his face look pleasant. No one truly looks happy or content unless something is going right on the inside.

42
One of Those Magic Moments

My mother was in the hospital about to have what we thought was a fairly routine operation on her throat. Though we all prayed very hard for her recovery and the success of the surgery, none of us realized the severity of the operation until we met with the doctor the night before. He told us it was a very delicate situation because my mother could come out of this operation never speaking again.

That evening before nurses took her to be prepped for the morning operation, a lot of tension and anxiety filled the hospital room. We all tried to remain cheerful, but know our concern showed through. My mother was as strong as I've ever seen her. I've never been prouder of her—or my younger brother Dale. Dale interrupted the conversation, "Mother, I would like to have you listen to something." He turned on the radio, and at that precise moment the D.J. was set up on the local radio station to say, "Mrs. Sanders, this is for you, from your family. We want you to know that we are all praying for you, and we also want you to know that God has got it all in control." At that moment he cued up and played B. J. Thomas's song "He's Got It All in Control."

As we sat there the tears flowed, and we all relaxed in God's presence and into the comfort of knowing that no matter what situation we face in life (even a chance of never speaking again or seeing your mother scared and your father just as scared for her), God indeed has us in the palm of His hand. He cares for us more than we will ever know or imagine. He loves us so much that He sent His Son to die for us. No matter what each of us face today, just like that moment in my family's past, He's got it all in control.

Why don't we give God the controls? He's waiting. I know as I look back at that evening in the hospital room, it was a magical moment for all of us, because God was there. One of my goals for this year is to make more magic moments in my family. Instead of just looking back and saying, "Those were the days," I want these to be the days. I want these to be the days for you, too. What can you do for another family member today to let him or her know that God has it in control, to let her know that you care enough to go to the radio station to get this all taken care of ahead of time and work out all the details. Do something for your brother, sister, mom, or dad. I know you can. Make a magic moment today. It will even be more special if you let someone know that God's got it all in control. He's waiting to take control— just give it to Him.

Revelation 3:20: "Here I am! I stand at the door and knock. If anyone hears my voice and opens the door, I will come in and eat with him, and he with me."

Let Jesus enter your heart and look what he brings with Him. Romans 5:1(TLB, *italics added):* "So now, since we have been made right in God's sight by faith in his promises, *we can have real peace* with him because of what Jesus Christ our Lord has done for us."

43
Measure Up

Have you ever felt as if people were always trying to get you to compete but you could never measure up to what they thought you should be? If so, you know just how the apostle Paul must have felt about his critics in the church at Corinth. This church was in a very wild pagan city, and the Christians there had a hard time getting things straight. At one point they started believing some false teachers, who had a lot of standards Paul didn't measure up to.

Paul describes the false teachers as behaving as though there were no standard of comparison higher than themselves; but Paul boasts only in the Lord (2 Corinthians 10:12–14). When he mentions the field that God assigned to him (v. 13), he talks about each of our own skills, strengths, and talents. He uses the example of a running field with different lanes in it (like the 220 or the 440).

Each of us has areas in which we excel. Let's concentrate on using our strengths and our God-given talents. Then we won't have to compare and we surely wouldn't have to compete.

Christians with hearts filled with Jesus Christ feel no need to compete with anyone. Instead, they continually look around to see whom they can pick up and pull with them. I once saw a special olympics in which a severely handicapped boy ran. He was way out in the lead and had a chance to win his first race. No one could believe it when he stopped and started to walk back. In the excitement everyone else missed another little boy who had fallen to the ground and was crying, hurt, and very embarrassed. The leader went back and picked him up. Together they walked across the finish line. No, he wasn't the fastest, and he wasn't the first. That day he didn't get a medal for winning the race, but the joy that must have filled his heart as he picked up another person will shine brighter and last longer than any award.

Psalms 89:6 asks: "For who in the skies above can compare with the Lord?" *No one!* Instead of comparing yourself with others, look at God. *How am I really measuring up in the areas in which God has gifted me? Am I using what I've got?*

We will never compare to Christ until the day we enter heaven, when we will be perfect. Even then we will be in awe at His glory and splendor. Until then, let's look at Him in such a way that we feel humble enough to need

Him, good enough because of what we have in our hearts to help others, but never too proud to look up. Let's continually be smart enough not to turn from side to side as we walk through school and life. Every time we look for someone else's approval, we really say that we need their approval more than we do God's. True strength comes from the Lord.

Don't miss out on this powerful, abundant life because you are looking at other people, instead of the very source of strength: Jesus Himself. Use Christ's standards as your measuring stick. "Measure up" to Him!

44
Me, a Millionaire?

Recently I heard the story of a young man in a mental institution who had inherited a million dollars and never knew it. Nor would he comprehend what it meant, if he were told. Can you imagine being a millionaire and not even knowing it?

Many people who hear this story say, "I wish it were me," "I sure would spend it, if I were that lucky," or, "If I had a million bucks, all my problems would be over." How would you act and feel about yourself if a million big ones just popped out of the sky into your lap, like that TV commercial? Would all your problems go bye-bye? Would you dress anyway you pleased, not trying to impress anyone? Would you feel free to be you, yourself, and nobody else? Most people think they would, but guess what? It's not true.

Studies show that people who inherit lots of money or win large lump sums are back to their original standard of living within three years. The money is blown, and they feel as miserable as ever. Why? Because they didn't have the skills necessary to earn it in the first place or the discipline to spend and invest it wisely.

Amazingly, most people who win a cool mil couldn't put half of it in the bank and never touch it. The interest alone would put you in the upper 2 percent income bracket.

Why is it hard to put half of a million in the bank for safekeeping and growth? Because it's nearly impossible for most people to put away half of their paper-route money, salary from the burger joint or department store, or even 10 percent of their weekly salary.

Take one minute and read Luke 16:10–12. This is God's law. Use wisely the little you have, and you will be given much more. Besides your money, what should you use wisely? List five things.

Now look up Luke 19:17 and see that God, like the king in the story of the talents, always rewards us for using what we have.

You are just like the man who doesn't know he has a million dollars. If you have trusted Jesus as your personal Savior, you have the ". . . unsearchable riches of Christ" (Ephesians 3:8).

Ephesians 1:18: I pray also that the eyes of your heart may be enlightened in order that you may know the hope to which he has called you, the riches of his glorious inheritance. . . .

Paul wants you to know just how rich you, as a child of God, really are. Go and act like you're worth a million. You know you are!

45
When I Need Confidence

Dear Bill: Things are going well in my life, but every now and then I get down and feel unsure about myself. Please help me find some reassurance in God's Word that will pick me up and give me confidence when I need it.

This young person's question shows a great deal of wisdom. Somewhere in the back of his mind, he knew that God has picker-uppers for us when we get down in the dumps. Since God is no better than His Word and He is incapable of a lie, the Bible is the greatest place in the world to look when you need a pick-me-up. When you want to start your morning with a few verses that will fill you with hope and give you confidence and strength, I've got some gems here:

Philippians 4:13: I can do everything through him [Christ] who gives me strength.

Hebrews 10:35, 36: So do not throw away your confidence; it will be richly rewarded. You need to persevere so that when you have done the will of God, you will receive what he has promised.

Philippians 1:6: Being confident of this, that he who began a good work in you will carry it on to completion until the day of Christ Jesus.

Habakkuk 3:19: The Sovereign Lord is my strength; he makes my feet like the feet of a deer. . . .

Romans 8:37: No, in all these things we are more than conquerors through him who loved us.

1 John 5:14, 15: This is the assurance we have in approaching God: that if we ask anything according to his will, he hears us. And if we know that he hears us—whatever we ask—we know that we have what we asked of him.

Isaiah 43:2: When you pass through the waters, I will be with you; and when you pass through the rivers, they will not sweep over you. When you walk through the fire, you will not be burned; the flames will not set you ablaze.

2 Corinthians 7:16: I am glad I can have complete confidence in you.

Proverbs 3:26: For the Lord will be your confidence and will keep your foot from being snared.

Ephesians 3:12: In him and through faith in him we may approach God with freedom and confidence.

1 John 3:21: Dear friends, if our hearts do not condemn us, we have confidence before God.

Isaiah 40:31: But those who hope in the Lord will renew their strength. They will soar on wings like eagles; they will run and not grow weary; they will walk and not be faint.

A friend told me about a row of pine trees that went between his house and his neighbors'. Because he wanted them to grow, he went to the tree doctor, who gave him strong liquid fertilizer. The tree doctor said, if he put it in the ground beside each tree, they would grow twice as tall in one season. By the end of the season they didn't grow just twice as tall; they grew almost four times larger than they would have normally. Later on he found out why. Unknown to him, his neighbor put some liquid fertilizer on the other side of the trees. A double dose when they needed it the most. They sprouted right up. Likewise a double and triple dose of God's Word from time to time will help give us a surge of strength and energy. Have these verses given you a lift and helped you grow a little today? I hope so.

46
The Romans Road

Just about every Christian has heard of the Romans road—the pathway of salvation outlined in the book of Romans. Many people have said that if they had the choice of just having one book of the Bible to live with forever, it would be Romans. We will go through this book to discover some exciting truths that can help each one of us feel better about ourselves and our position in Christ. It may help you rediscover what a wonderful gift you have in salvation, lead someone else to Christ, or make a decision for Jesus yourself. For the first time you may realize just where you have come from and where you are going.

The Romans road goes from our sin state to being saved in Christ. Romans 1:16 is its start: "I am not ashamed of the gospel, because it is the power of God for the salvation of everyone who believes. . . ."

When Paul states that he is not ashamed of the gospel, he means he is proud of it and will stand on it until death, if he has to. One thing, more than anything else, should be the bottom line for everything we do in our lives: God's Word. God is no better than His Word. He is just and true. He is incapable of lying. If He says it, it must be. Why should we be proud of the gospel? Because it is the power for salvation of everyone who believes.

In my Bible I have 3:10 written in the margin right by Romans 1:16. This way I know the verse that comes next, when I am sharing with someone. "As it is written: 'There is no one righteous, not even one." Beside that verse I have 3:23: "For all have sinned and fall short of the glory of God." These two verses merely show that every single person who has ever lived—other than Christ—has sinned. I doubt if you can find any person who can say that he or she has really met someone who has never, ever sinned or made a mistake. Besides putting our faith in the gospel, we must all realize we have fallen short of God's glory on our own. If a person can't recognize that he has made mistakes and has sinned on his own, he will never recognize the need for Christ.

The next verse that I have in the margin is 5:8: "But God demonstrates his own love for us in this: While we were still sinners, Christ died for us." These are amazing and powerful words. While we were still sinners, God sent Jesus Christ to die for us. Not because we were good enough, not because we earned it, but because He loved us that much. Whenever you wonder about God's love for you, remember this: He loved you even before you turned to Him and even when you were turned *from* Him.

From Romans 5:8 I turn to 6:23. This pivotal verse shows us the two ways in which we can go in life. Even though we know that we are sinners, even though we know Christ can save us, even though we know that God loved us so greatly, we still have a decision to make. That decision leads to a destiny. "For the wages of sin is death, but the gift of God is eternal life in Christ Jesus our Lord."

This verse has two parts. The first deals with the wage—a payoff, something we earn by our actions, something we earn and deserve by our way of life. "For the wages of sin is death. . . ." *Death* here means "spiritual death." The payoff for living in our sin and not doing anything about it is eternal separation from Christ. It is called hell. The other part of this verse is beautiful: ". . . but the gift of God is eternal life in Christ Jesus our Lord." Notice the word *gift*. It is the opposite of the word *wage*. A gift is free; you cannot pay for it. You can only be thankful because of it. Someone must buy a gift. Christ paid for our gift of salvation, by dying on the cross. We cannot earn it, nor can we be good enough to keep it. Just like a gift at Christmas, God's gift of eternal life or salvation is free—and it's also for anyone who will ask.

Romans 8:28 promises: "And we know that in all things God works for the good of those who love him, who have been called according to his purpose." If we love God, we accept His Son. If we have been called according to His purpose, He touches our hearts, we discover Christ for ourselves, and we ask Him to be our personal Lord and Savior. God's Word says all things that happen to us will work out for good. You see, He will give us the creativity and insight to find the good in everything that happens to us. When negative and terrifying things happen to us, we will realize what God wants us to learn through them. How exciting to know that as a child of God every single thing in your life is planned! All that happens has a purpose, and there is beautiful goodness in it.

To make sure you have this beautiful thing called salvation, to be in the right heart state, to realize that all things that happen to you in the future will work for the good, do what it says in Romans 10:9: ". . . Confess with your mouth, 'Jesus is Lord,' and believe in your heart that God raised him from the dead, [and] you will be saved." God only requires two things: First, He wants you to tell someone that Jesus is the Lord of your life. Second, you have to have faith in that. If you truly believe in your heart that God raised Him from the dead, you *shall* be saved.

I think God did not have video machines back when Jesus was alive because He wanted us to have total faith in things like the virgin birth and the death on the cross. Even seeing Christ's suffering and love in person doesn't prove everything. Thomas, who had been with Jesus for three years, had to see before he could believe in the Resurrection. He had to feel the nail holes; he had to feel Christ's hands and side. We, too, must have faith. If we believe He was raised from the dead and say, "Jesus is my Lord," we shall be saved.

Once we confess Christ and believe in His death and resurrection, we have this beautiful gift called salvation, but the Romans road doesn't stop here. Romans 12:1, 2 tells us how to live as a Christian: "Therefore, I urge you, brothers, in view of God's mercy, to offer your bodies as living sacrifices, holy and pleasing to God— which is your spiritual worship. Do not conform any longer to the pattern of this world, but be transformed by the renewing of your mind. Then you will be able to test and approve what God's will is—his good, pleasing and perfect will."

In those verses God covers all four areas of life: physical, spiritual, social, and mental. God shares how we should grow as physical people: " . . . Offer your bodies as living sacrifices, holy and pleasing to God. . . ." Because they only hurt God's temple, we do not choose to put drugs, alcohol, and tobacco into our bodies.

We should also become " . . . holy and pleasing to God. . . ." God wants us to live so that our spiritual beings (the way we conduct ourselves) please the Lord. Notice this means pleasing to *God* and not necessarily to *us*.

"Do not conform any longer to the pattern of this world. . . ." We are social creatures, but God wants us to realize that His salvation makes us different from the world. If we have Christ in our hearts, we are saved. Anyone who rejects Christ is not saved. God does not want people to sit on the fence.

Revelation 3:15, 16 warns: "I know your deeds, that you are neither cold nor hot. I wish you were either one or the other! So, because you are lukewarm—neither hot nor cold—I am about to spit you out of my mouth." God says that if we are in the middle, thinking halfway about living like Christians and living in the world the other half, He would just as soon spit us out of His mouth. God wants us to be dedicated.

God covers the mental when he says to renew your mind. God's Word is so important, because it keeps healing, renewing, building, and strengthening us. God's Word is our sunshine, the rain that helps us grow, and the very energy that keeps us alive.

There you have the Romans road. You can turn to these pages any time you need to lead someone to the Lord. Once he has heard these things, he must make a decision. All he needs to do is say a simple prayer, stating in his own words that he realizes that everyone is a sinner, including him. He must recognize that God's Word says if he stays in his sin state, the wage of this sin is death. Show him that he needs to ask God for this beautiful thing called eternal life, recognize that what He did on the cross covers the sin, accept what He did, and ask Him into his heart as his personal Savior. What a wonderful gift you could give someone . . . the gift that is free . . . the gift of eternal life.

Next time, when the road you are traveling seems rocky and things are not going well, turn back to the Romans road and walk through a few of its steps to realize just how fortunate you are!

Just fill in the blank with your name. "I, _____, realize that I have sinned many times and hurt You, God. I am very sorry. I've read Your Word and know that You died for my sins. You paid the price for each and every one of my sins. I'm sorry for hurting You. With your help, I'll live for You the rest of my life. Please come into my heart and be my Lord and Savior for ever and ever. I love You, Jesus. Amen."

47
We Need Each Other

In the speaking profession I am my friend John Crudele's mentor. He is a gifted speaker who specializes in helping people say no to drugs. For the past few years, we've shared over the phone, in person, and through the mail, and I listen to his talks and tell him where he can improve. He also listens to mine.

During one of those exciting moments, I helped John with the final words of his speech to parents. He tells about how his dad did so many beautiful things with him as he grew up. John remembers the way they looked for Christmas trees, how his dad told him stories at night, gave him dreams and goals to shoot for, got him excited about reading and going to libraries and museums. As he shares these memories you can visualize his dad right there with him, going through all the motions. John didn't quite know how to finish the talk, but it came to me in a flash. I suggested, and every single time he now uses the phrase "go make some memories." It is also the title of his talk.

Just recently we went skiing in Colorado. We were on some pretty treacherous hills, and John is a better skier than I am—with a lot more guts. He looks like a miniature version of the hulk, and his attitude and confidence carry right on through with his theme, even on the ski slopes at thirty miles per hour. While we were in Vail, Colorado, John became *my* mentor and encourager for the entire day. He kept me going and talked me through the tough hills. He told me to visualize getting my hands downhill, attacking the hill, and seeing myself complete it with success. At the end of the day we realized that we need each other in different roles and at different times of our lives. I couldn't have made it through the day without him, and he shared how many times his speaking career wouldn't have been where it is today had I not helped him in my areas of expertise.

I'll bet you have a friend whom you've helped out many times, encouraged, been there for when he needed you. But at times when you needed help, maybe you've never called on your friend. Maybe he doesn't think he can return the favor. Maybe he doesn't feel deep down inside that he can truly help you the way you have helped him. Ask him. Let him know that you need help.

Use nine powerful words, from another of my mentors, Art Fettig, to start a new relationship withyour friends: "I've got a problem, and I need your help!" People like it when they are needed. We all need to be needed. Please focus on the following verses that explain what two can do and how two are definitely better than one:

Ecclesiastes 4:9, 10: Two are better than one, because they have a good return for their work: If one falls down, his friend can help him up. But pity the man who falls and has no one to help him up!

48
Short People

About ten years ago a song entitled "Short People" put them down. It even claimed they had no reason to live.

My little girl, Emily, is the smallest student in the entire elementary school. She is in kindergarten, and she is smaller than anyone there. Her self-esteem will depend on how people act toward her and how she reacts. If they call her names, she will find it very difficult to accept and put up with.

We usually call people names and use put-downs when they are different. I asked my little girl about two neighbor girls who are black. I said, "Are they different?"

She said, "Yes."

"Are they bad?"

"No. They are neat people, Daddy. I really like them." We

found out that different is just different. It is not bad, scary, or frightening; we need not talk down or get angry at something just because it's different. We can choose to wallow in our differences or to make the best of them and be creative.

A very short man in the Bible had a goal he didn't think he could ever reach. Zacchaeus wanted to see Jesus. What did he do? The people were too tall and the crowds were too thick, so he climbed a tree. That is creativity. As Jesus passed by, He looked up and said, "Come on down." Guess what? Zacchaeus jumped on down. Of course, many people didn't like it (like the Pharisees, who nagged, yelled, and put down the shorter man), but Jesus didn't mind. He knows that different is only different, not bad, because He created different. Christ's purpose on earth was to meet our needs, save us from our sins, no matter if we are tall or short, black or white, introvert or extrovert, good or bad. He came to save all of us who are sick in sin.

Watch out for put-downs. If you are short, think of Zacchaeus. Look up, and you won't be short at all.

Luke 19:1–10: Jesus entered Jericho and was passing through. A man was there by the name of Zacchaeus; he was a chief tax collector and was wealthy. He wanted to see who Jesus was, but being a short man he could not, because of the crowd. So he ran ahead and climbed a sycamore-fig tree to see him, since Jesus was coming that way.

When Jesus reached the spot, he looked up and said to him, "Zacchaeus, come down immediately. I must stay at your house today." So he came down at once and welcomed him gladly.

All the people saw this and began to mutter, "He has gone to be the guest of a 'sinner.'"

But Zacchaeus stood up and said to the Lord, "Look, Lord! Here and now I give half of my possessions to the poor, and if I have cheated anybody out of anything, I will pay back four times the amount." Jesus said to him, "Today salvation has come to this house, because this man, too, is a son of Abraham. For the Son of Man came to seek and to save what was lost."

By the way, I'm teaching Emily how to climb trees.

49
It's Not Fair!

Why am I always getting in trouble for something I didn't do? I always get the blame!

I don't think I should get in trouble for the things my brother does. You never think he does anything wrong.

I never seem to be able to do what you want me to do. My brother does everything right and is never wrong. He was the firstborn, and dad told me one time that he only wanted one child and that I wasn't wanted—I was an accident. It isn't fair.

Do any of these letters I have received from teens sound familiar? I am sure they do, if you have a brother or a sister. No matter if they are older or younger, at times it seems parents always side with brothers or sisters. When I was growing up, it seemed as if my siblings could do no wrong.

Your parents need you to share with them in a loving matter, when they favor others, so they can see if they are being unfair. Quite often it is just a matter of focus. We easily concentrate on our brothers and sisters getting their way and magnify the fact that we don't get our way.

Have you ever heard someone say: "No one ever said life was going to be fair"? Actually all of us should be glad that God is not truly fair and strictly just, because if He were, none of us would reach heaven. When Christ died for our sins, He paid for them. It is impossible for us to measure up in God's sight, so He sent His only Son, a perfect, unblemished lamb, to take over where we could not. He paid the penalty that would keep us out of heaven forever.

David is a perfect example of how to act the next time you feel your parents or anyone else is being unfair. Read Psalm 71.

Psalms 71:20, 21: Though you have made me see troubles, many and bitter, you will restore my life again; from the depths of the earth you will again bring me up. You will increase my honor and comfort me once again.

50
The Company You Keep

When I grew up, I remember my grandma saying, "Watch the company you keep. Tell me the company you keep, and I'll tell you who you are." Companions are very special persons. Though we are supposed to like everybody, to love everybody, and try to get along with everybody, our companions and friends are special. They influence us for good or bad. I can walk through the mall and go by all kinds of people whom I don't know. Maybe I pass hundreds of people, and none of them influence me to be good, bad, or indifferent. But my friends influence me a great deal by the way they talk, whether or not they steal, if they cheat on tests or not, if they swear, if they drive fast and don't use their seat belts, and so on. Because I spend time with my friends, I identify with them. Whether or not I like it, I become part of them. They also influence me for good when they challenge me do to something better or say, "I love you," to my parents.

I strongly challenge you to get help for a friend who has a drinking or drug problem. You will fall into that same problem if you hang around with that person long enough. If a friend of yours steals things, don't let it go along unchecked. If you've got a friend who has a deep inside hurt from a childhood pain, help him talk it out to a counselor or someone who can help him work through it. If you've got a friend who doesn't know the joy of having the creator of the universe living in her heart, help her find God's Son!

"I am a friend to all who fear you, to all who follow your precepts." In that psalm (119:63) David described himself as a companion (a friend) of all those who feared the Lord; he liked people who feared God. By the way, *fear* means "respect and honor." To believe, love, respect, and honor someone means you fear him. It means that you believe he will keep his word. Don't think of fearing God as a negative. When you fear Him, you love, respect, and honor Him.

Do all your friends fear the Lord? Which ones are you so impressed with, while you are with them, that you work very hard to make sure you can go out together, have fun together, and party hearty with? Do they fear God? Do they love Him? Do they respect Him? Do they honor Him? If not, you are keeping the wrong company. You certainly wouldn't want to work for a company where, as soon as you put its name on your résumé, no one else would want to hire you. It is the same with friends. They help you develop your life and act out what you really believe and harbor in your heart. Choose your friends wisely. Make sure you are in a good company!

Which of your friends would you send to a job interview to represent you? Which ones would you want to take with you if you had to talk to God personally?

51
When Times Get Tough

What do you do when times get tough? Who do you turn to? Do you get tough back? Do you know where your strength lies?

Like me, I'm sure you have witnessed many people who have had severe handicaps, been in accidents, seem to have everything going against them, yet they seem to be the most cheerful people in the world. They always put a smile on someone else's face. They don't dwell in their own misfortunes and waste time on self-pity. Depression seems to elude them because of their daily activities.

I wanted to find out what one of the superstars in the greatest book of all time did when his enemies were after him. He had hidden and lived in caves, an outcast hunted down like an animal, ready to be murdered at any time. What did David do? We find his answer in Psalm 63. He said that to know God and His kindness was more important, more beautiful, and more precious than life itself. David's greatest and deepest desire was to develop his soul—to become pure in the sight of God, to become righteous, to truly live, think, and breathe in a way that would please God—to be God's friend.

A great saying, "God can take the place of anything, but nothing can take the place of God," is especially true in times of trouble and despair. Look at how David responded when the world gave him a ton of trouble. "O God, you are my God, earnestly I seek you; my soul thirsts for you, my body longs for you, in a dry and weary land where there is no water," cried his heart (Psalms 63:1). When David hurt, his heart cried out that he longed for God. He wasn't bellyaching and feeling sorry for himself. Instead he knew the true secret in satisfying our hurts: crying out to God.

In Psalms 63:2, 3, despite the pain he felt, David rejoiced, "I have seen you in the sanctuary, and beheld your power and your glory. Because your love is better than life, my lips will glorify you." David remembered exactly what God's love was like, so he glorified Him. He didn't just store up memories of the bad times, but kept in his mind the beautiful things that God had displayed. He continues, "I will praise you as long as I live, and in your name I will lift up my hands. My soul will be satisfied as with the richest of foods; with singing lips my mouth will praise you. On my bed I remember you; I think of you through the watches of the night" (Psalms 63:4–6).

David knew that God would win in the end. Verse 11 shows what will happen if we, too, truly long for God: "But the king will rejoice in God; all who swear by God's name will praise him, while the mouths of liars will be silenced."

How exciting to read the Bible and know that God wins

in the end! I hope seeing His victory gives you the same walking courage it gives me. It helps me walk through anything life throws at me. When you hurt, use your memory and seek God with all your heart. Be like David in Psalm 63.

52
Am I Worth It?

Have you ever thought about what it costs your parents to raise you? *Newsweek* ran an article that shared the cost of raising a child to the age of eighteen in America. Look at these figures, and if you are like me, you will be a little startled at the cost of raising you.

The total cost adds up to almost $135,000.00. It breaks down like this:

Shelter	$ 9,000.00	
Utilities	$ 4,700.00	
Food away from home	$ 4,500.00	
Food at home	$17,900.00	[That's a lot of pizza]
Household	$10,200.00	
Grooming/miscellaneous	$ 5,600.00	[No wonder the bathroom door is always locked]

Recreation	$ 9,500.00
Clothing	$ 7,200.00
Transportation	$24,900.00
College (four-year private)	$40,000.00

These figures were provided by the Urban Institute and the College Board. Reprinted, by permission, from GROUP Magazine, copyright 1987, Thom Schultz Publications, Inc. Box 481, Loveland, CO 80539.

Kind of amazing, isn't it? Almost $135,000.00 is the cost to raise you to be eighteen years old. Of course, we haven't even mentioned the four or five years' worth of hours your mom and dad have spent physically holding you, changing you, rocking you, hurting with you, laughing with you, crying with you, and being with you. We never mentioned any of the thousands and thousands of hours in which Mom and Dad prayed for you, cared about you, wondered how you would act in a situation and desperately pleaded with God to guide you through this venture or an event. When you add it all up, it is quite a total. Are you worth it? God thought so. That is why He gave His life, so you could live forever and ever. Your parents or guardians must think so, or they wouldn't keep on keeping on.

In God's eyes, as well as your parents' eyes, you are definitely worth it. Sometime today, tell someone "thank you"—but first tell God.

Romans 8:38, 39: For I am convinced that neither death nor life, neither angels nor demons, neither the present nor the future, nor any powers, neither height nor depth, nor anything else in all creation, will be able to separate us from the love of God that is in Christ Jesus our Lord.

Proverbs 3:13: Blessed is the man who finds wisdom, the man who gains understanding.

53
A Worthy Hero

An eleven-year-old boy named Jimmy Masternado, who was in fifth grade in Ohio, was praying one day and seeking God, when it came into his mind that the state of Ohio had no motto. California had the motto, *Eureka*, "I have found it," and Jimmy wanted his state to have a motto, too. He thought the motto of the state of Ohio should be "All things are possible with God." Jimmy went to his mom and said, "Mom, how can I get the motto of Ohio to be 'All things are possible with God?'"

She said, "Go away. Go away. I don't know. Don't bother me."

He came back and said, "Mom, how can I do it?"

Finally she said, "Well, write to the editor of the newspaper."

So Jimmy wrote to the editor, who told him he would have to go before a congressional committee, get a petition, and get it signed. Jimmy went before a couple of congressmen and explained his purpose. He got the petitions and started getting them signed. He went door to door everywhere, even to the state of Ohio's dedication of a building. He walked up to the governor and said, "Governor, would you please sign this petition so the motto of Ohio will be 'All things are possible with God?' " The governor signed it, and Jimmy went on to get more and more petitions signed.

Finally, the day came when Jimmy had all the signatures. He stood before the joint congressional body of that state— this is a fifth grader! I can see those men looking down at that kid, wondering what he was going to ask for (a lobby on peanut butter or something?). This little fifth grader got up and said, "I think our motto ought to be 'All things are possible with God'!" Then he proceeded to tell the men why he thought so. They were so impressed that they passed it unanimously. Today Ohio's motto is "All things are possible with God"! Not bad for the fifth grade. Don't say, "God, I can't serve you until I get older." Jimmy didn't. I hope you don't forget those six powerful words: All things are possible with God.

In my opinion, Jimmy is a worthy hero for each of us because he attempted something great for God. His dream turned to reality because he put his feet under it and did what he had to do. He got the petitions. God will hear your prayers, also, if you become a hero in His name. You're never too old or too young to serve God.

Psalms 66:16–20: Come and listen, all you who fear God; let me tell you what he has done for me. I cried out to him with my mouth; his praise was on my tongue. If I had cherished sin in my heart, the Lord would not have listened; but God has surely listened and heard my voice in prayer. Praise be to God, who has not rejected my prayer or withheld his love from me!

It kind of seems as if Jimmy spoke the words in each of these verses!

54
Do I Have to Move?

Every year thousands of families have to move. Job relocations, plant closings, a better territory, a broken family—there are hundreds of reasons. Many times teenagers get caught up in the shuffle.

When I was a sixteen-year-old sophomore, my father relocated to another town, which meant we had to move. I had gone to a very small high school, where I felt really comfortable. The school I moved to was ten times as large, with a thousand more kids. *What did I do wrong that caused us to move*, I wondered, until my dad told me it was scarey, but he wanted to make it because the opportunities ahead would be better for all of us. My family moved in the middle of the summer, but not me. To finish driver's training, I stayed with a friend, and I wanted to remain there through my junior and senior year. I just couldn't imagine moving away from my hometown, my roots, my comfort zone. I felt afraid, expected the worst, and imagined every kind of fearful thing. But nothing awful happened. The worst event I experienced was taking two and a half weeks to find my new locker. (Many people say that I am exaggerating, but I am not at all.) I knew one fellow when I moved there. We rode the bus together in the morning and took it home together at night. Because all the kids, all the rooms, the different floors, and so on overwhelmed me, I kept my books with him and didn't even worry about finding my locker until the third week of the school year. By then my friend had gotten sick and tired of my taking up all his space.

If you have to move, think of the new opportunities and friends it will provide. Yes, you feel sad about leaving old friends behind, and it is scary to make a change, but life is full of changes. Only when we change do we grow. If we stay the same we get stagnant.

As I look back, I can clearly see that outside of my family, the major things that shaped my life happened because of that move. The jobs I took in my new town helped me grow and expand far beyond anything available where I used to live. Several key people who have influenced my life greatly only came into my life after that move. College, traveling through the United States, painting parking lines with my friend Steve, and many more opportunities opened to me because of the different geographical area we moved to. By the way, my dad was in his fifties, and the move definitely frightened him as well. He moved, earning no more pay, but because he moved, just ten years later his retirement benefits were forty times greater than they would have been had he stayed in the little shop where he worked for over thirty years.

Yes, it can be scary to move, but it is just like life . . . if we don't move, we stay in the same place. Kind of like coasting . . . sometimes you feel you are doing a good job and you can just coast along. You have worked hard at your studies, but now you plan to rest and take it easy. Remember, you can only coast downhill. You can't even do it on flat ground for very long, or you will stop. Then if you don't get going again, you will not be able to improve or grow at all. Coasting takes the momentum you build up by going down the hill.

If you or a friend have a move in your future, make the best of it. *Look ahead.* Don't concentrate on what you are losing or leaving behind. Get excited about the new opportunities and people waiting for you.

Proverbs 3:5, 6: Trust in the Lord with all your heart and lean not on your own understanding; in all your ways acknowledge him, and he will make your paths straight.

55
Is My Movie R Rated?

"I'm doing all right." "I'm not ashamed of my life." "I'm no angel, but I'm not as bad as many others I know."

Many people feel as if they only need one life goal: "enjoying life." According to them, the main thing is to have fun; to be happy; to do what you want, because you've worked hard, and you deserve it.

What if you sat in a movie theater and watched a movie of your life. As you watched the scenes, suppose someone— Jesus—was sitting right beside you. How would you feel as you watched what happened last weekend or saw the thoughts in your mind as you lusted after someone? How about the angry thoughts, the unfairness that you projected toward a brother or sister, the way you acted and reacted around the house and didn't help out unless your mom threatened you within an inch of your life? How would you feel as He saw you looking over someone's shoulder on a test? How ashamed and how embarrassed would you be?

If I had to watch my movie, I know most of my life would be a disaster. I would feel like cringing and crawling into my own shadow—hiding forever and ever. What do you have to change in your life so when Jesus comes back you won't have to have Him worry about watching the R- and X-rated portions of your life? How can you change these things?

1. Make a list of them.
2. Pray about them.
3. Purpose in your heart to do something about them.
4. Do it. Make the change!

You can better your life any time you want. You can ask for God's help whenever you want. No one will do it for you. No one can make excuses for you, either. You've got to do it yourself.

The disciples did not believe it when Jesus said He was coming back. After He was buried, they hid in the upper room. Even when Mary said she had seen Jesus, and He was alive, they called her a liar and said she just exaggerated. But before they knew it, He stood in the room with them. He had come back just as He said He would. After staying forty days, He went back to heaven in the midst of them. Before He left, He warned, "I'm coming back even yet." Do you believe it? He said it could be any moment and any day—not so that you would give up on life and wait for Him on a hilltop, but so you could make the changes that you need to make.

If the movie was entitled You, what would it be rated? If it is R or X right now, change it before He returns. You still have time!

James 5:7, 8: Be patient, then, brothers, until the Lord's coming. See how the farmer waits for the land to yield its valuable crop and how patient he is for the autumn and spring rains. You too, be patient and stand firm, because the Lord's coming is near.

56
Why Can't I . . . ?

Many parents receive a letter similar to the following while their son is in his first career or first year at college:

Dear Mom and Dad: I am really enjoying myself and learning many new things, but I must ask you some questions. Why can't I do many things, like my friends? I am the only one here who doesn't know how to balance a checkbook or go shopping. I had no idea that $10.00 bought so little. I have also noticed I keep running out of money before everyone else, because I never learned anything about a budget. The other day I made a fool of myself when I tried to run the washing machine and drier. These term papers are so difficult. In high school I could wait until the last minute, and when I got in a jam you would help me type them the night before they were due.

Please do my little brother a favor. Let him experience the things I have been sharing with you, so he doesn't have to write this letter when he gets to college. I do appreciate all you did for me, but looking back, I realize that you did a little too much. I love you! Your son.

Because I don't want you to write the same letter to your parents someday, I ask you to learn to do things on your own, experience different things, and handle situations instead of asking your parents to do that for you. Many parents love their teens so much that they don't want them to go through the same pain and agony that they did; but their love overshadows the fact that teens will never (and can never) learn unless they experience things themselves.

Take responsibility around the house. Look for things to do. Don't wait until you're told or begged. Don't wait until your parents get angry because you have waited so long. Become someone who is proud of his accomplishments. Become a capable person. Don't just *say* that you will help around the house—*start* helping!

Budget your money and time. If you have a term paper due in three weeks, look at a calendar and mark off ten days, so you can work on it an hour each day. It will get done on time, and you will learn a lot more. Accepting help from your parents is okay, but sometimes teens become helpless because they don't do enough for themselves.

The Lord has given you many gifts, abilities, and talents. Use them, or someday you might lose them. If we use our gifts, abilities, and talents, the Lord will help us multiply them. Read the parable of the talents in Matthew 25:14–30. It will help explain this principle. God gave one person five talents, another two, and another one talent (v. 15). The person with five talents traded them and made another five. Likewise, the person with two talents gained two more. "But the man who had received the one talent went off, dug a hole in the ground and hid his master's money" (Matthew 25:18).

To the two people who took what they had been given and used them, the Lord said, "Well done, good and faithful servant! . . ." (v. 21, 23). To the one who buried his talent, the Lord said, "Take the talent from him and give it to the one who has ten talents" (v. 28).

We can come to a very simple conclusion: Both our human and financial investments grow when we invest them.

57
Appreciation, Not Anger

Pat Vance was seven months old when his leg was amputated because of a birth defect. I read his story in Tim Stafford's book *The Trouble With Parents*. Pat said that many times he felt self-pity, but most of the time he made the best of things. He even had a few laughs with his artificial leg. Once during a kickball game his leg fell off right at the point of contact, and it went all the way to the pitcher's mound. Another time it fell off right in the hallway while he was walking from class to class. During the beginning of each year he would freak out the new kids by reaching down to adjust his socks and turning his leg backwards.

Fifteen separate times Pat went into the hospital to have a special operation in which doctors cut the bone back so it wouldn't grow through the skin. Each time he was laid up for three months. But instead of sensing anger, when I read

Pat's story, I heard a great deal about appreciation. He appreciated his father, a quiet man who had a very nice job but quit that job when Pat was just a baby. For an entire year he took no pay, while he tinkered and worked on a new leg for Pat. He made a better leg than the one they had received from the hospital, with the leather, steel, and braces. Pat's father made a leg that fit just like a shoe, with no contraptions. Each year he worked on another one. As Pat's other leg grew he needed another anyway, and each and every model became a little better, a little easier to use, and a little nicer looking.

Throughout Pat's entire story, I heard him say that his father never complained about the price of each operation—sometimes $2,000.00 to $3,000.00. His father never complained about the hard work and the hours he spent earning the money for the operations and designing each new leg.

All of our parents have sacrificed for us in many ways, but it is very easy to notice the areas in which they need improvement, instead of being thankful and appreciative for all that they have done. Take a moment today and instead of getting angry over an area that might trouble you, communicate that love and appreciation to those people who love you more than anyone in the world—next to God, that is.

Psalms 139:13, 14: For you created my inmost being; you knit me together in my mother's womb. I praise you because I am fearfully and wonderfully made; your works are wonderful, I know that full well.

58

"Stop Picking on Me"

Dear Bill: . . . No one likes me. They always call me names and pick on me. I try to ignore them, but I can't. You don't know the pain I feel. I just want to be accepted . . . .

I get letters like this one almost every week. Each and every time I speak at a high school, several people tell me the pain of being picked on. If you feel like this, follow these steps to help yourself:

1. *Learn to ignore it.* If you give people a payoff (crying; getting mad; running to your teacher, parents, or principal; or merely letting them know you are bothered by their words), they will keep on bugging you. I know it's hard to do, but you *must* ignore it.
2. *Realize they are immature and usually possess low self-esteem.* People like to pull others down to their level, because somehow it makes them feel better. Don't let others use you as a doormat or the butt of their jokes.
3. *Get busy.* Stay active and involved. If you have goals to reach and people to help you, you will walk faster and feel better about yourself. In my book *Tough Turf,* I list twenty-

five steps you can take to enlarge your self-esteem until you feel good enough about yourself to laugh at yourself.

4. *Focus on the people with you.* Luke 9:50 tells us: ". . . Jesus said, 'For whoever is not against you is for you.'" If five teens pick on you, remember that the other three hundred in your school are on your side.

5. *Laugh at yourself.* One teen told me he had a better putdown about himself than anyone else. The others would call him a name, and he would say something twice as bad. (Read Matthew 5:40, 41.)

6. *Love your enemies.* You may win them for Christ. Read Matthew 5:43–48 and see what it has to say. Matthew 5:44 commands: ". . . Love your enemies and pray for those who persecute you."

7. *Get creative.* Look for new ways of making your enemies into friends. Two bullies were calling a little guy in on a fight. The little fellow drew a line on the ground and said to the biggest one, "I dare you to step over that line!" He did. Then the little guy put his arm around the big guy and said, "Good. Now you are on my side!"

8. *Pray for them.* Pray for their very souls. You will then see them as God does: lost, hurting, and alone. When you see them as God does, you'll feel love instead of anger.

If you need a friend, you've got one in God and me. Write me and I'll talk to you through the mail. My address is in the back of this book.

Remember why a pigeon pecks on the wall—to get a piece of corn. He will keep on pecking as long as he gets the payoff. If the corn stops, he'll get tired of pecking. People who are angry and hurting inside will stop picking on you if you stop the corn. Sounds corny, doesn't it? But it works.

59
You Cost Me $700.00

In 1978, when I was a brand new speaker, I had just read Zig Ziglar's *Confessions of a Happy Christian*. Zig is one of my greatest heroes and mentors in the speaking profession and life. He taught me to live off-stage what you teach on stage and how not to be a hypocrite; how to look yourself in the mirror everyday and see your best friend, someone you're proud of and not ashamed of; what it's like not to look over your shoulder and to worry about what anyone says about you.

I had read Zig's account of how he had stood up for his faith, and as a result several speeches had not gone his way, because they didn't want a professing Christian to speak to them. A few months later I found myself in the exact same situation, with a large company. I had given them two presentations and wanted to do more. When they called me into the office, they told me that of the fifty evaluations from the people in the two groups, two said I had too much religion. (By the way, in each of these three-hour sessions I spent less than four minutes mentioning that it is important to have a spiritual foundation, and I never even mentioned the word *Jesus*.)

That day one man said, "If you promise never to mention God again and to say nothing about religion or being spiritual, I will give you seven more talks." I felt as though Satan himself stood right in front of me, tempting me—just like many of the martyrs down through history—never to mention Christ and not to tell people where I get my strength from or what true success and happiness are all about.

I looked at that man, and remembered the chapter in *Confessions of a Happy Christian* where Zig tells how he lost a talk but left with his dignity intact. I stood up, watching my friend Zig do the same, shook the man's hand, and then the hand of another man, who held the calendar with those seven speaking dates (it would have been the largest contract I had at that time), and I said, "I respect you for where you stand, but I also want you to respect me. I cannot come in here and tell your people how to be successful and give them the ten steps to success, but leave out the greatest one. I don't want any of your people to think I am successful, happy, or can handle life because of my biorhythm or astrological sign, or anything else that people rely on. They've got to know that they can be successful in all areas of their life, and I don't think that can happen without God. As you know, I do it very tactfully, and I share my faith around humor and around stories. I always say, 'This is what I believe,' not, 'You should believe. . . .' I am not ashamed of what I have done, but I am going to have to decline these seven talks. I am sorry. . . . Good-bye."

I went home. All the way, I could only think *God, You just cost me $700.00.* I kept talking to myself, saying, *If this is what standing up for You is all about, I am going to go broke by being a Christian.* As you can see by my attitude and my talk, I was very young in my Christian walk, because I didn't have the confidence that God always comes through, that He will never let us stand on our own.

I got home, head bowed low, and told my wife what had happened. Right then the phone rang and it was: Guess who? The man from the business! He said they had been talking about me, and they believed that my faith was real, and he wanted me (all of me) and my material (all of my material) presented to his people. He gave me those seven talks—and three others. Isn't that the way that the Lord works? He always throws in a bonus if we stand up for Him!

He'll give you bonuses in your life as well: peace, happiness, security, and confidence. Not the confidence you get from racing someone, being faster, stronger, taller, smarter, or better looking, but the kind you get from knowing deep inside that God (your God) is in control. He won't cost you. The only cost is the price the people pay when they don't know the Lord; it is called anger, hurt, and pain and being alone when everyone abandons you. Because of what we've got in our hearts—Jesus Christ—we will never be alone.

If you stand up for God, He will stand up for you! You can never outgive God!

Matthew 10:32, 33: "Whoever acknowledges me before men, I will also acknowledge him before my Father in heaven. But whoever disowns me before men, I will disown him before my Father in heaven."

Don't ever be ashamed of God.
If you are, you should be ashamed.

60
Answered Prayer

Does the Lord really answer prayer? Quite often we don't believe He does, so we don't pray with much confidence. When you are in need or desperate, prayer comes easily; but to pray as a way of life, even when things are fine, and to know deep in your heart that God hears you and will answer you, is a beautiful thing.

One night I gave an after-dinner talk to some business people. My normal comfort zone is teens, parents, and teachers, so I felt a bit nervous speaking to a bunch of business people. After a long cocktail hour (I mean a *real* long cocktail hour), there was a group of definitely drunk people in the back of this room, which held about one hundred. The drunks were loud and boisterous, and they wanted everyone to know it. I started and talked about eight to ten minutes, but this group still would not get quiet. They would not shut up; they would not have any courtesy at all, and they made life miserable for me. In their laughter and jeers, the talk was getting muffled. Just about the time I got ready to put them down and say something smart like, "Give me my chance to talk now, and you can talk later," or, "Would one of you like to stand up and give us a report about the meeting you are having right now," or, "Do you desperately need something else to drink? If you do, there is a bar across the street," I leaned on the podium, which was small and made out of tin, sitting on top of the table. As I did that the podium crashed to the tabletop, in about five different pieces. It broke the ice in such a way that the head of the group went over and asked the loud table to be quiet. I fixed the podium, we had a good laugh, we talked about making the best of negative situations like the one I was in, and the rest of the talk went wonderfully. Just a little while later, I realized that the podium breaking was a gift from God. He allowed me to hold my tongue—not to put someone down. He came to my rescue in an amazing way.

I don't believe in coincidences—especially not for God's children. He watches over us, and He knows every hair on our heads. Do you think He wants me to look bad in front of a group, especially when it is my livelihood? Absolutely not! Do you think that He wants you to make a fool out of yourself in front of your friends? No! He wants us each to be a strong stage person for Him—a witness—someone who makes other people say, "I want to be like you. Where do you get your strength from?" God allowed me to do that in an amazing thing called breaking the podium at the right moment.

Look in your past. I think you will see that if you asked, God came to your aid and rescued you right when you least expected it and when you most needed Him. Count on Him today to do the miraculous and amazing. That is what He is there for!

Mark 11:23–25: "I tell you the truth, if anyone says to this mountain, 'Go, throw yourself into the sea,' and does not doubt in his heart but believes that what he says will happen, it will be done for him. Therefore I tell you, whatever you ask for in prayer, believe that you have received it, and it will be yours. And when you stand praying, if you hold anything against anyone, forgive him, so that your Father in heaven may forgive you your sins."

Matthew 21:22: "If you believe, you will receive whatever you ask for in prayer."

Luke 11:9, 10: "So I say to you: Ask and it will be given to you; seek and you will find; knock and the door will be opened to you. For everyone who asks receives; he who seeks finds; and to him who knocks, the door will be opened."

61
Write Your Parents

Dear Bill: I just can't talk to my parents. I feel as if I don't know them and they don't know me. When I start to communicate with them, we argue or get upset. I never say what is on my heart. What can I do?

Write it down. The beautiful thing about writing instead of talking is that you'll get all of your feelings out in the open, cover all of your thoughts, and express all the points that you want to get across, and you'll do it without interruptions and having to listen to another person sharing, which causes you to lose your train of thought.

If you've got feelings for someone (especially parents, a

brother or sister, or even God), write them down, then give them to that person. Let him read it. If he does not feel comfortable talking back to you, have him write back. My wife and I learned this technique years ago. It is called dialoguing. You write down exactly how you feel on a certain topic. A great topic to start with is "What I admire most about you." For ten minutes, you write all the things you admire about the other person. She also sits there, writing what she admires about you for ten minutes. Then you exchange papers, read them, and for five to ten minutes you talk about them. This will open up and clarify your true feelings for each other and help bond your friendship and love like very few techniques I have ever seen.

In school you often can choose how to do book reports: You can say it aloud or write it down. Life is the same way. Communication is too special and too important for you to let it go by unchecked, unpracticed, and unsaid. Remember: If it is hard to say something in spoken words and you are unsure how it will come across, write it down. It is worth the extra effort. Go ahead and share a piece of your heart with someone on paper.

People who say, "My heart's not up for grabs," lead very lonely lives. What we "give away" most times, ends up what "we got"! It's like that between us and God: "No one has ever seen God; but if we love one another, God lives in us and his love is made complete in us" (1 John 4:12). When we give His love away, we get more back.

God Himself shows us that if we truly want to communicate with someone special whom we love, we will try different methods. "One night the Lord spoke to Paul in a vision: 'Do not be afraid; keep on speaking, do not be silent'" (Acts 18:9).

God *spoke* to Paul, but He used fire when communicating with Moses. "There the angel of the Lord appeared to him in flames of fire from within a bush. Moses saw that though the bush was on fire it did not burn up" (Exodus 3:2).

147

God's creativity and sense of humor never cease; He reached Balaam through a *talking donkey:* "Then the Lord opened the donkey's mouth, and she said to Balaam, 'What have I done to you to make you beat me these three times?'" (Numbers 22:28). Jacob was reached by a dream sent from God. Read about it in Genesis 28:10–22. Angels were even used to communicate for God. Mary was comforted and told her glorious news by an angel. "But the angel said to her, 'Do not be afraid, Mary, you have found favor with God'" (Luke 1:30). God also used handwriting on the wall. This was the best way to grab Belshazzar's attention (Daniel 5:5–9).

Grab your parents' attention and hearts, but don't blame me if they object if you mark on the wall. . . .

62

Too Busy Cutting Trees

When I was associated with the Dale Carnegie courses, I heard a story about a boy who went up north to work in a lumber camp, cutting trees. He had great promise, great strength, and they thought he would be one of the all-time great tree cutters. The first day he cut fifteen trees, the second day twenty trees, the third day twenty-two trees, and so on. By the end of the third week he had cut almost thirty trees a day—more than anyone else in the history of the company. But for the next two weeks, the number of trees that he cut each week dwindled: twenty-five, twenty-four, twenty, fifteen, twelve, and finally eight. The foreman came over to him and asked, "What is the problem?"

"I don't know."

"Are you working as hard?"

"Of course. I even get here early. I don't take any breaks. I even chop all through my lunch hour."

"Are you swinging the ax as fast?"

"I'm even swinging it harder than ever before."

Finally the foreman looked down at his dull blade, ran his finger across it, and asked, "When was the last time you stopped to sharpen your ax?"

The young boy looked surprised and replied, "Sir, I don't have any time to sharpen my ax. I've been too busy cutting trees."

Have you ever noticed how easily you can get so involved in whatever you're doing that you end up doing it for weeks, months, and years, only to realize that you haven't stopped to sharpen your ax—whether it be with physical fitness, mental fitness, spiritual sharpening, or social sharpening. Perhaps in school you get so bound up in work that you forget to better yourself with relationships with people or God. Many working people hate their jobs, because they have stopped growing. They've gotten the job, and they keep it by showing up every day, but they never really change or grow. Because of that, their lives aren't as fulfilled as they could be.

How can you sharpen your ax? First of all, take inventory. Look at your skills. Who are you? Next set your sights on a goal. Aim. Yes, shoot for the stars that are highest in the sky and brightest in the night. Even if you miss those stars, you'll hit the moon. Many people fear shooting for big goals or having exciting dreams because they've been told they will fall flat on their faces. The only people who give you advice are full-time face fallers. They are good at failing because that is all they talk about. They have practiced it and memorized it in their minds, as well as in real life. They keep saying that you can't do it.

Don't get so busy with life that you fail to see the importance of improving yourself. Each year, set your sights on new achievements, new goals, and new heights to reach. What do you do as soon as you reach an exciting goal and people clap and applaud and you feel good inside? You have two choices. You can stop and say, *Well, I've done better than most. Who would criticize me for resting and taking it easy?* No, I don't believe that is you. Before you completely reach a goal, set another one. Set your sights on new skills and new sharpening tactics. With the right resources (God, your parents, key community members, a brother or sister, great friends, caring adults who know you and believe in you, and so on), you can do anything—that is, of course, if you stop cutting just long enough to look down and say, "Ooops, I've got some sharpening to do." Take time to "tune up," then the length you go will be longer!

Proverbs 27:17: As iron sharpens iron, so one man sharpens another.

63
Scared Sexless

Turn on TV and you're likely to see a special on AIDS. I watched one entitled *Scared Sexless*. In it Indy 500 winner Danny Sullivan, known for his playboy life-style, said he never has sex without using condoms. Heisman Trophy winner Eric Dickerson told how he had made it through his AIDS test and jumped for joy because he didn't have the virus.

Several other singles were interviewed, giving comments such as: "I insist all my men use condoms," "I believe in living with a person for a while to see if the shoe fits before we consider marriage," "My mother said if she had had more sex before marriage, she probably wouldn't have divorced my dad."

What do these comments and the openness of these so-called superstars do to you? They astonish me! Nowhere in many of these specials do they talk of the moral issue of sex before marriage, low self-esteem, guilt, abortion, total selfishness, and God's rules!

Read how sex outside marriage is sin before God and how pain and punishment often follow. Go to 2 Samuel 11:2–5 and look at David's "if it feels good" attitude. Now look at how amused God was with this sin; read reality in 2 Samuel 12:1–14.

It's your choice: the pace of the world or the peace of God. Notice what David did in 2 Samuel 11:2–4.

Verse 2: He saw a very beautiful woman bathing. (Was he in God's will, watching another man's wife taking a bath?)

Verse 3: He found out she was married. (Did he have respect for her then? *No!*)

Verse 4: He sent for her and had sex with her. (Her moral standards were just as low as his at this point, but God had blessed him tremendously in the past. He knew God and he knew better!)

God said to David in 2 Samuel 12:9, "Why did you despise the word of the Lord by doing what is evil in his eyes?" In verse 11 He continues, ". . . Out of your own household I am going to bring calamity upon you." If you ever consider committing adultery, don't forget:

Proverbs 6:25–27, 29: Do not lust in your heart after her beauty or let her captivate you with her eyes, for the prostitute reduces you to a loaf of bread, and the adulteress preys upon your very life. Can a man scoop fire into his lap without his clothes being burned? . . . So is he who sleeps with another man's wife; no one who touches her will go unpunished.

I wish David had been scared sexless because of God's Word. The rest of his life would have been a lot less painful. How about you?

Let's not have safe sex before marriage—let's save sex for marriage!

64
Peace in Prison

I met him in prison, when I talked to around twenty-five inmates about the importance of a positive attitude and the need for Christ in our lives. One quiet old man back in the corner didn't say anything during the entire meeting, but life, love, and peace radiated about him. After the meeting, I asked if we could talk on the way back to security. There I would show the mark on my hand under the infrared light and be let out. There I would say good-bye to my new friend.

He asked me, "You know where we're at, don't you?"

I said, "Prison."

With over twenty years of prison life in his voice, he responded, "No. We're in a can of hell with the top ripped off. We can't look out—we can just look up. If we didn't have people like you guys and Jesus Christ, we wouldn't have anything to look up to."

"But you have such a peace about you. How do you do it?"

"If I thanked Jesus with every breath I take, I couldn't thank Him enough."

I went to that prison to help some inmates, and one of them showed me a peace that passes all understanding. Though I went to meet some strangers, instead I made a friend. I saw what the love of our mighty Lord can do in a life, if we will let him.

Learn from this godly man. Notice how he focused on the good people in his life, instead of his troubles. He was looking up at God, not down at his troubles and worries. It wasn't fake. You could sense his love for God from the other side of a room.

Does anyone even know you are a Christian? Do your actions show what your heart believes? Read Acts 16:22–28 to see how if you have your eyes and heart in the same direction as Paul and Silas while they were in prison.

Acts 16:25: About midnight Paul and Silas were praying and singing hymns to God, and the other prisoners were listening to them.

65
Communicate Well

Good communication can help you in school, in your career, and anytime you address an audience or speak with friends. Follow these Ten Commandments of Good Communication to make a big change in your life:

1. *Be accurate.* Violating this rule can really get you into trouble.
2. *Be brief.*
3. *Be clear.* Avoid complex word combinations—phrases that have double meanings or parts that might be misunderstood.
4. *Don't try to impress your audience.* Speak in terms they can understand.
5. *Consider your audience.* Whenever you write or speak, use language that clearly shows your audience that you know who they are.
6. *Think and organize before you write or speak.*
7. *Make your message interesting.* Say something worthwhile, then dress it up with a little humor, some anecdotes, a story or two, and so on.
8. *Don't leave out essential facts.* Remember the five Ws: Who, What, When, Where, and Why—and How!
9. *Be ethical.* Be fair with everyone whom you work with in any type of communication. Always give credit where credit is due. (For instance, I got these commandments from my good friends at Business Professionals of America. Jody VanCooney assembled a booklet entitled "Verbal Communications: File of Ideas.")
10. *Don't just relate it—illustrate it.* Use actual objects, models, movies, photos, and drawings whenever you can.

Even though you may never give a formal speech, address a large audience, or accept an award, you still need to know these tips. Lack of proper communication skills is the number-one cause of divorces and bankruptcies. Family and business failures happen because people do not communicate properly.

If you have the chance to give a talk, remember the greatest communicator of all time: Jesus. Did He just give facts, or did He share the most powerful tool known to mankind—accurate, powerful storytelling? He was accurate, brief, clear, and He talked in terms His audience could understand. Jesus used everyday objects for examples, was always organized, and made His talks very interesting—at times thousands of people followed Him. He invented the word ethical, and He sure knew how to illustrate it.

Why not take a look at one of His famous parables and see how it can apply to your life? (Read about the rich fool in Luke 12:16–21.) There is a phrase in there that shows up quite often in today's language. ". . . Take life easy; eat, drink and be merry" (v. 19). Notice what God says immediately after that statement—two words: "You fool!" Jesus is not condemning money itself, but He realizes it is one of the greatest hindrances to spiritual growth—unless it is as dedicated as our life must be. Then it can make an influence in promoting the kingdom of heaven. Remember this powerful statement: "A man's true wealth is that which is still possessed when all that death can take is taken." God has communicated very clearly and accurately. Let's listen to His wise words when we hear them. Filter His Words through your head and place them in your heart.

Luke 12:19, 20: "And I'll say to myself, 'You have plenty of good things laid up for many years. Take life easy; eat, drink and be merry.' " But God said to him, 'You fool! This very night your life will be demanded from you. Then who will get what you have prepared for yourself?' "

66
A Brother Like That

Recently I heard about a fellow whose brother came into some money and bought him several very nice gifts. He shared how generous and loving his brother was, and a young teenage boy overheard the conversation. Afterwards what do you suppose the teenager said? How do you think he finished the sentence, "I wish I . . ."? I would have said, "I wish I had a brother like that," or, "I wish my brother was that nice to me."

This very wise young fellow responded, "I wish I was a brother like that." Instead of wanting his brother or other people to give him things and to be nice to him, he wished he had the character to be that kind of person. That is what we call real wisdom. You can have wisdom like that if you want it, but you have to ask for it. You have to seek it out. You have to talk to God and desire it. His Word is very clear:

Proverbs 2:6-12: For the Lord gives wisdom, and from his mouth come knowledge and understanding. He holds victory in store for the upright, he is a shield to those whose walk is blameless, for he guards the course of the just and protects the way of his faithful ones. Then you will understand what is right and just and fair—every good path. For wisdom will enter your heart, and knowledge will be pleasant to your soul. Discretion will protect you, and understanding will guard you. Wisdom will save you from the ways of wicked men, from men whose words are perverse.

During the next few days, when you look at people, notice how they act and react. See if they can cry and love others. Watch and see if they are filled with generosity and if they can stoop to help a child. You will also notice people who are too busy doing their own thing, worrying about themselves too much to help another. Then ask yourself, *What kind of brother would I like to be?*

67
Our World of Instant Stimulation

"I'm bored."
"There's nothing to do."
"There is never anything worth watching on TV."
"That was a boring movie."
"Do you want to come over to my house and goof around?" "Not if there's nothing to do."

Being bored and having nothing to do seem ways of life for many people. How can we combat it? Have you noticed how everything today is instant? Instant coffee, instant tea, instant this or that. Take the microwave for instance. Everyone lives by it, and you are out of date if you don't have one. The microwave oven is a great convenience. What about television? You hold a remote-control channel changer in your hand, popping buttons one right after the other. By the time you get done with twenty or thirty of them, what do you say? "There's nothing on." Each television show, the experts say, has about five seconds to catch your attention, or you are gone. If it doesn't grab you in an instant, you say good-bye.

What about the movies? You go to the theater to see a picture that cost about $11 million to produce. Many, many thousands of dollars went into each five-minute portion of the movie. But if it doesn't grab your attention, the movie is a flop. If it does, they make millions.

Comedy is the same thing—short, fast quips with punch lines intended to grab you and make you laugh. It doesn't matter if the material is X rated, below-the-belt putdowns, or whatever. If it works, it works; if it doesn't, it doesn't.

Caffeine—we grab a Mountain Dew or a Coke so we can get a buzz, stay up longer, and do homework.

Relationships are even instant. Meet someone today and have instant sex tonight. The world shows it, the TV portrays it, the movies say, "If you don't do it, you're square," and all the ads on TV make you feel like a creep if you don't keep up with the superstars, the high-visibility people.

No wonder we all feel bored. Everything is instant. If someone doesn't have the same computer or the same games you are used to, you don't visit him anymore. It's hard to be creative. It's hard to make up a game. It's hard to pretend and use your imagination today. The sad thing about it is when you grow a little older and you have to pretend and be creative, you will not have that skill in your bag of "life skills."

Instant stimulation! To combat it:

1. *Get back to the basics.* The next time you and your friends go out, don't use anything that is mechanical or has a motor on it. Pretend. Use your imagination. Go cross-country skiing. Find things to do that will force you to be creative.

2. *Each day write in a journal and describe your feelings.* Get to know you. You will refer to this in a few months or years, and it will be one of the greatest friends you've got, because you will have put in the effort to learn how to enjoy life and what it takes without having to depend on something or someone else to stimulate and motivate you that instant.

3. *Talk to your parents about changing the house around a little bit.* Try to turn off the TV for at least an hour and a half each night. Have each person in the family do homework, read, get creative with some art, build something with his or her hands, draw, paint, or just have quiet discussions around the house.

Does it sound crazy? Are you laughing at me already? Do you see what I mean? We've been brought up in a time where we've let a small group of people who program our TV and movies tell us what to do and how to live, what's cool and what's not, and if you don't do this or that, then you are out. I don't like to be in the minority, but I am. When I go to a restaurant with my friends and none of us order drinks, quite often the waitress looks at us and laughs and says, "Okay" as if to imply, *You've got to be kidding. You think you can have a good time tonight without getting drunk? You think it's possible to have a good time without putting chemicals or substances that can hurt and harm you into your body and system?* Well, listen close, world: *Yes, I do!*

Not only do I believe it's possible, *I know it's possible.* For twenty-seven years I knew what it was like to put things in my body that made me forget the reality of the moment in order to have fun, and I know what has happened the last ten years of not putting those things in. The kind of fun I have been having lately is much more beautiful and long lasting, with no hangovers, no regrets; I never have to look over my shoulder or wonder who is catching me in this lie or that, and neither do you, if you will only do things God's way.

We always get back to that, don't we? Isn't it funny that no matter how old you get, where you live, what you look like, or what you do for a living, God has His rules, and they benefit everyone. You don't have to believe it. All you have to do is enjoy it. God set it up that way.

Instant stimulation: The greatest thing to combat that is patience. Unfortunately, if you keep enjoying instant stimulation, you never develop patience.

James 5:7–11: Be patient, then, brothers, until the Lord's coming. See how the farmer waits for the land to yield its valuable crop and how patient he is for the autumn and spring rains. You too, be patient and stand firm, because the Lord's coming is near. Don't grumble against each other, brothers, or you will be judged. The Judge is standing at the door!

Brothers, as an example of patience in the face of suffering, take the prophets who spoke in the name of the Lord. As you know, we consider blessed those who have persevered. You have heard of Job's perseverance and have seen what the Lord finally brought about. The Lord is full of compassion and mercy.

68
Love Us the Same

One of the hardest things for parents to do is not to play favorites among their children. Have you ever felt like this:

Dear Mom and Dad: There have been so many times in my short life when I have felt alone or like leaving you and never coming back because I really don't think you understand me. You two always say it was the same with your parents, when you were younger. You never hear what I have to say. Just because I am the oldest doesn't give you the right to look at me first when anything is broken or missing. It always seems to me that you are harder on me than my younger brother.

Dear Mom and Dad: You may not notice it, but it seems that you spend more time with my brother than you do with me. I know you have told me he needs more attention, and that I am so independent that I don't need any attention, but that is because I got used to being by myself through the past several years. I like being independent, but I also like to receive the attention you give my brother. Please listen to my cry.

Dear Dad: Just because I'm your stepson doesn't mean you have to ignore me and never spend time with me. We could be a great team, if we could develop love.

Have you ever had the nerve to ask your mother and father if they love you or your brother or sister more? That is a hard question to ask, and an even harder one to answer. It is also not a very wise question to ask. The reason is simple: Parents *should* love all their children equally, but there is something wrong, because most don't. If one parent is outgoing and likes sports, it is hard not to show favoritism to the child who is also good at sports and talks to people without fear.

I have warned two or three of my friends who were very active in sports in their high school and college days not to put that kind of pressure on their children. They should also love them just the same, even if they don't do the exact same things and live up to their image. But just the other day it happened to me. About a foot of snow had fallen, and my wife and I went sledding with our two little ones. When our five-year-old came, she was too afraid to go down the hill. She felt intimidated and wanted to start off slowly, then jump up to the pace that we had been working at for about an hour. When she wouldn't go down the hill and merely wanted to sit and watch us and laugh with us, I grabbed her, put her on the sled, and gave her a push. It scared her half to death. She put out her feet and hands and stopped the sled, crying. She didn't talk to me most of the rest of the day. I also gave her verbal abuse when I said things like: "You sure are a sissy," and, "I can't believe you're afraid of such a little thing as this. Look at your little brother and sister. They are not afraid. How come you are?"

Boy, did I have some work to do when I got back to the house that afternoon. The Lord zapped me right where I was, and I went and asked her forgiveness. I told her how sorry I was for trying to make her into something that she wasn't at the moment.

When I start to put undue pressure on myself or anyone else, I like to look at it in the right perspective. What if she were paralyzed, lost, or stolen. I wouldn't care at all if she went sledding down that hill with us. Just to have her near me, smiling and laughing, would answer my every wish. Since she was there, I took her for granted and wanted her to be just like me at that age.

When you feel as if your parents don't love you or love another brother or sister more, you hurt. It is okay to go to your mom and dad and share this with them. Tell them how you feel and how you love them and need their encouragement, time, and love. They will never know unless you tell them. By learning about favoritism now, you can save yourself a lot of pain through relationships, as well as with your own children, in the future. Look at how family favoritism resulted in friction and jealousy; read Genesis 37:3–35.

69
The Wrong Kind of Laughter

Several years ago I went to the library with a prayer in my heart. I wanted to come up with a poem that would depict all the different ways and different types of people whom we put down in school. As I sat there, God gave me each and every one of these verses within about an hour and a half. I have never studied this, but had it instantly memorized. I present it in each and every student assembly I give.

It's wrong to put down—
The new student, the poor student,
the one who walks funny and talks funny.
Let's call him skinny and call her fat,
and, "What kind of shirt do you even call that?"
"Hey, giraffe, how'd you get so tall?"
and, "You're so short you've got no place to fall."
Check out buckteeth, and look at those ears,
"Hey, elephant nose, why all the tears?"

And the one with no friends, she eats all alone,
bet we could make her cry all the way home.
Let's laugh at that guy, he got cut from the team,
"You're the worst player we've ever seen!"
And she was too chicken to stay with the play,
"It's 'cause she talks funny and forgot what to say."

I heard his parents both left home,
"If you weren't adopted, you'd be all alone."
Hey, her mother's real sick, oh, that's too bad,
"Don't wait around for us to be sad."

Look who's coming, it's crater face,
I'm glad I don't have zits all over the place,
"You're just a loser, you'll never win,"
and, "How dare you come to our school,
with the wrong color skin?"

Yes, we're the populars, we have to be cool,
and as you've seen, we can sure be cruel.
But as long as you do all the things that we say,
you, too, can be privileged with our group to play,
but there's no security being part of our team,
we even turn on our own, as you've probably seen.
But if you're cute and handsome and really smart,
why, you'll fit in right from the start.

But you must never disagree,
And for heaven's sake, don't turn ugly,
or we'll kick you out, right into the street,
for us to be popular, we'd even cheat.

We don't believe in the things from above,
like honesty, integrity, and brotherly love.
Society's taught us to be number one.
Who cares if you're hurt? We're having fun.

It's not just students we pick on each day,
but anyone who's different and gets in our way.
Society has taught us, don't worry what you say,
and forget the consequences past today.

We also pick on teachers who are old and shy,
and we love to make the bus driver cry.
And the cook, last week we threw food right in his
face,
and the counselors and subs we love to disgrace.

And of course the principal we always boo;
it's nothing personal, just the thing to do.
And there's Mom, whom we're mad at, and Dad, who's
unfair,
of all the nerve, yesterday he even asked me to move a
chair.

I've covered them all, so I'm ready to stop. . . .
But wait, there's one more, I almost forgot,
It's my dear, charming brother, who puts chips in my
pop. . . .

Please help me wipe out the wrong kind of laughter in
your school, where you work, and in your town. Together,
we can keep sadness and pain only on the six o'clock news

and not in our own backyards. In Matthew 25:40 Jesus taught us much more clearly about the wrong kind of laughter: "'. . . I tell you the truth, whatever you did for one of the least of these brothers of mine, you did for me.'"

70

A Christmas Gift— Cancer?

One Christmas, I couldn't understand why my father was sick. The doctors said he would not make it through the week, the cancer was too thick in his stomach, and he could not be operated on. A year later, I knew all this came about so our family could be healed and brought together. In that sickbed, I saw my father accept Jesus Christ as his Lord and Savior. Two months later he walked the aisle of our church and joined the church with my mother—both in their seventies. About a month after that, on one of the neatest days of my life, I saw them get baptized. My younger brother and my older brother made up and became friends and said, "I love you," for the first time in a long time. For the first time in over twelve years I cried. Three older sisters whom I love dearly shared things they had been feeling about one another, hurts and pains and forgivenesses, that would never have been brought out otherwise. My family, restored and strengthened, stopped taking God's blessings for granted at least for a little while. We couldn't see the good at the time, but as I look back I can see it all.

If someone in your family is physically sick or hurting or emotionally scarred, pray. Let the Lord be your strength and remember there is good in there somewhere. Dig in and find it. It may be in an unfamiliar package, but once you unwrap it, you'll find His "gift."

Isaiah 55:8: " 'For my thoughts are not your thoughts, neither are your ways my ways,' declares the Lord."

Romans 8:28: And we know that in all things God works for the good of those who love him. . . .

71
Stop the Jeep!

Have you ever thought about the times in your life when God directly put His hands on you or intervened in a situation to keep you alive or made a significant change in your life because of the turn of events that followed? Have you ever wondered why you took one road and not the other?

Many times God puts His hand on our lives, but we don't

see it until later on. God makes it clear to us that He truly sent one of His angels or His very hand reached down from heaven and touched us and pulled us this way or that.

Something happened to me a number of years ago, but I didn't see God's hand in it until many years later. Two friends of mine and I were driving in my friend's Jeep on a rainy summer night. All three of us had been drinking heavily, going from bar to bar. We were five minutes from the next town, on gravel roads, in lower Michigan, going about eighty miles per hour. Time and speed mean nothing, and neither does life, when you are under the influence of alcohol or drugs. All of a sudden my friend in the backseat said, "Stop the Jeep. I've got to go to the bathroom."

We shouted back, "No way, it's raining outside. We'll be in town in five minutes."

"Stop the Jeep!" To this day I don't know why we stopped. There was no reason to stop—two against one. It was raining, plus it had been a long time since we had seen a grown man wet his pants. On this pitch-dark evening, full of big black clouds, with rain coming down, my friend got out to go to the bathroom. All of a sudden we heard a rumbling, deep growling noise at the bottom of the hill. He got back into the Jeep, and we inched our way down the hill. Less than 200 yards down, at the bottom of this gravel road, a freight train crossed the road. The only warning for this railroad was an old and battered sign. We would never have seen it in time; we would have crashed into the train, at a high rate of speed.

That night we just laughed. We were shocked for about five minutes, but then never gave it another thought, and we went on destroying brain cells and taking the chance of killing three or four innocent families and possibly ourselves. Several years later God clearly pointed out to me that He had His hand in it, reaching down from heaven and stopping the Jeep. He caused my friend's heart to change, and he willingly stopped.

Now I know that at certain times God will actually cause

a miracle to happen and intervene in our lives. The sad thing is that we have to see so many marvelous miracles today, because of TV and videos and all the wonderful things that they do in movies, in order to be impressed with God for very long. God told Noah to build an ark, and he obeyed. God spoke to Abraham and told him to leave his hometown with all of his home furnishings, and Abraham obeyed. He didn't need ten miracles, fireballs from heaven, or rubies and diamonds popping out of the earth. He heard God's voice, and he obeyed. Later God told Abraham to sacrifice his son Isaac, and he obeyed. Once again God's hand came down from heaven and grabbed Abraham's arm and He said, "Stop. I merely wanted to see where your heart was."

Please take a moment to think about an event in your life in which God played a big part. Maybe you haven't thanked Him or have forgotten how much He loves you. Today, stop long enough to give Him that thanks by way of your actions and a renewed spirit and heart.

James 1:17: Every good and perfect gift is from above, coming down from the Father of the heavenly lights, who does not change like shifting shadows.

72
May I Have Your Autograph?

I'm one of those lucky people, who because of my profession as a full-time speaker, receives many standing ovations (they're glad it's over), and I'm often asked for my autograph (to see if I can write). It's hard to feel bummed out when people clap for you or look at you, saying, "That was the best speech I've ever heard." (When they say that, I know it's the *only* speech they've ever heard.)

Many years ago I learned a lesson about giving autographs from one of the greatest speakers in the world, Zig Ziglar. He told me never to sign my name without giving credit to the one responsible: Christ! Because of that I try never to write my name without putting a Scripture reference beside it. Now when I autograph my book *Tough Turf* I put "p. 67" beside my name. That's the most important page in the entire book; it's my story of coming to know Christ as my Savior on Christmas Day, 1978. In my parents' book, *(Almost) Everything Teens Want Parents to Know,* I write "p. 73" beside my name, because it explains step by step how easy it is to turn one's life over to Jesus.

I remember telling Zig one day how much I admired him for showing me how to live and witness for Christ. I looked to him as an idol, and he stopped me right there and told me never to look up or down to any man or woman. Only look up to Jesus. He will never fail or leave me. He could have said, "Yeah, I am something great, ain't I?" Instead, he gave the glory to God.

Never go around with a big head about yourself. "Pride goes before destruction, a haughty spirit before a fall" (Proverbs 16:18). (Notice how you almost always lose the game of tennis, ping-pong, checkers, or Trivial Pursuit, right after you brag about winning so many in a row.)

Jesus' cousin, John, was being asked for his autograph when he spoke to standing-room-only crowds. Instead he gave us the formula for keeping our heads small and life in its proper perspective. Read about it in John 3:27–30. The key verse is verse 30. Is it true of you?

73
Green Eyes

Dear Bill: My boyfriend is jealous of me, and he gets so angry if I even look at another guy. What should I do? I feel like I'm in prison. He gets so upset that I worry about what he might do someday.

My dear friend has a very serious problem. If a boyfriend is that jealous of her, it shows serious insecurities, and she needs to ask why he is her boyfriend. However, if she has strong feelings for him and would like to approach him with a suggestion and possible solution and see what choice he makes, I can offer some help.

A story in the Bible tells about jealousy and anger and gives some very wise counsel. However, this jealous guy didn't take the counsel and ended up letting his anger result in murder. Of course it is the story of Cain and Abel.

Both brothers brought offerings to God, but God did not accept Cain's. Cain became very jealous of Abel's offering. Cain got angry, even though he had been at fault in bringing the wrong kind of offering. The amazing thing is this: God came to Cain as this girl can come to her boyfriend. In Genesis 4:6, 7 (TLB) He warned: ". . . Your face can be bright with joy if you will do what you should! But if you refuse to obey, watch out. Sin is waiting to attack you, longing to destroy you. But you can conquer it!"

Cain had a choice, and so does that boyfriend. His girlfriend has a choice too. No relationship can last if the reins are pulled so tight because of jealousy. If she cannot look at other people while she's young and talk to other people so she can learn how to communicate with people of the opposite sex without getting her boyfriend so mad, angry and jealous, it is a bad situation.

Think of God's suggestion to Cain and ask yourself: *How do I react when someone suggests I have goofed up? Do I deny I have a problem, or do I try to find a solution for it?* God gave Cain a chance to correct his mistake, but Cain refused. Cain's story shows us what can happen to a life and how it can be ruined forever by wrong choices and continued sin. If someone, especially a parent or teacher, points out that you have done something wrong and you need to change it, I challenge you and beg you to take God's way instead of

Cain's way. Don't be a wandering fool, like Cain. He ended up a nomad the rest of his life.

Cain's story is told in Genesis 4:1–17. You can also read about him in the New Testament, Hebrews 11:4; 1 John 3:12; and Jude 11. But for now, concentrate on the gentle and encouraging word God gives Cain to help set him straight. He may be speaking to you in a special area of your life now as well. Go back and read Genesis 4:7 again!

74
The Story of the Pump

Have you ever seen a water pump—a hand pump with a long handle? You can learn a lesson from this pump, because it is actually the lesson of life. I heard this lesson for the first time with my enthusiastic friend Zig Ziglar. He was clinging and clanging that pump as he told the story of life.

Zig told how some friends of his were out in the country and very thirsty when they spotted this old pump. One went over and started pumping the handle as hard, fast, and as wildly as he could. The other friend said, "Don't you know that first you've got to prime the pump?" That is just like life. You've got to put some water in before you can get water out. They primed the pump a little bit, and they pumped some more, but no water came. Right about then his friend was ready to give up when he heard, "You've got to keep on pumping. Don't give up now. The water is way down deep. In fact, the deeper the water, the cooler, the tastier, the more beautiful, and the more satisfying it is. That is just like life. Once you start on a project and work on it for a while, it is easy to give up, because you don't see results right away. But success is just around the corner. You've got to keep working at it. Don't give up! Perseverance —it's called stickability. Keep at it!" The man grabbed that pump handle and kept on pumping. A little while later the water started to come. After it began, it came like a flood—cool, refreshing, and beautiful tasting water. At that point, he noticed an amazing thing. He did not have to pump as hard, fast, or furiously. Just easy, steady pressure kept the water flowing at full force.

In life, once you work hard to get something going, a little regular effort keeps it going. If you work on a project and it's hard to find the answer, you dig and dig. Finally all the material comes, and before you know it, you've got enough for ten term papers, just because you kept on studying and looking.

Don't give up once you get the momentum going. If you've got a project facing you today, remember the lesson from the pump. Prime it first, dig in, and then work with all your effort and might. Use every ounce of energy, strength, and imagination that you can come up with. After the answers start flowing, stick with it. If you are on a regular reading program, don't give up. Read a little every day. If you are doing some exercising, do a little every day. If you are growing spiritually and are in good tune with the Lord, don't give up. Memorize a verse a week. Five minutes of Bible study a day will keep the waters of spiritual growth flowing in and out of you. If you've got some good friends (you've worked hard to get them and put a lot of effort in to make those friendships real and strong), keep building those friendships regularly.

Remember the story of the pump. In all your relationships and every area of your life (mental, physical, spiritual, and social), pump hard at first, prime it often, and keep the momentum going.

Philippians 3:12: Not that I have already obtained all this, or have already been made perfect, but I press on to take hold of that for which Christ Jesus took hold of me.

75
The Pain of Leaving

Dear Bill: I am excited about going away to college. My parents have helped me select the school; we visited it together; and I am leaving in a couple of days. It seems as if, along with their excitement, they are also very sad, because my mother cries a lot these days. I heard Mom and my dad talking about how much they would miss me and the pain they were going through, even though they were excited. It is hard for me to truly enjoy myself, knowing that they are hurting. Is this normal? Signed: A concerned son.

I guess you will only realize what it's like to have a son or daughter leave you when you become a parent and your child leaves. I've talked with many parents, and they have told me a son or daughter leaving home is one of the most painful times in life. They felt as if they had a part of them ripped off and torn apart. Sure, you'll come back to visit, but you have left the nest, are learning to fly, and in your excitement you may only rarely say, "I love you," "Thank you," "I'll never forget you," and, "I am what I am because of what you did for me."

I think it is important for young people to realize that they can make that time easier on their parents by preparing them little by little. While you are growing up, encourage your parents to let you go away for weekends with your friends. Always call them and keep in touch when you are out late at night. Take trips in the summertime with your buddy. Your parents will get used to your leaving a little at a time if they experience this along the way.

Before you go to college, communicate with your parents. Let them know that with God and all they have taught you, no problem will ever be too great. Parents go through enough pain during this difficult time. Try to make it as light as possible. Ease their load as they have eased yours while you were growing up. Let them know that you are ready to fly, but you will always be a phone call or a visit away; and you will never take for granted what they have done for you or the love they will always have for you. As you "let go" you'll hang on to the Lord who made you. ". . . If God is for us, who can be against us?" (Romans 8:31).

When Jesus was dying on the cross, leaving His mother, He eased her pain by asking His closest friend to be near her and call her mother:

John 19:26, 27: When Jesus saw his mother there, and the disciple whom he loved standing nearby, he said to his mother, "Dear woman, here is your son," and to the disciple, "Here is your mother." From that time on, this disciple took her into his home.

If you have any questions or problems you wish to share, please drop me a note at:

Bill Sanders
P.O. Box 711
Portage, MI 49081